Winter Season

Florida A&M University, Tallahassee
Florida Atlantic University, Boca Raton
Florida Gulf Coast University, Ft. Myers
Florida International University, Miami
Florida State University, Tallahassee
University of Central Florida, Orlando
University of Florida, Gainesville
University of North Florida, Jacksonville
University of South Florida, Tampa
University of West Florida, Pensacola

Also by Toni Bentley

Costumes by Karinska

Sisters of Salome

Holding On to the Air, by Suzanne Farrell with Toni Bentley

TONI BENTLEY

WINTER SEASON

A Dancer's Journal

University Press of Florida

Gainesville · Tallahassee · Tampa · Boca Raton

Pensacola · Orlando · Miami · Jacksonville · Ft. Myers

Copyright 1982 by Toni Bentley
Preface copyright 2003 by Toni Bentley
First cloth printing 1982 by Random House, Inc.

First Vintage Book edition 1984
2003 paperback edition by University Press of Florida
Printed in the United States of America on acid-free paper

08 07 06 05 04 03   6 5 4 3 2 1

Library of Congress Cataloging-in-Publication Data
Bentley, Toni.
Winter season: a dancer's journal / Toni Bentley, with a new preface.
p. cm.
Originally published: New York : Random House, c1982.
ISBN 0-8130-2705-5 (pbk. : alk. paper)
1. New York City Ballet. 2. Ballet dancing. 3. Bentley, Toni. 4. Ballet dancers—
United States—Biography. I. Title.
GV1786.N4B46   2003
794.8—dc22   2003057917

Grateful acknowledgment is made to the following organizations for permission to
reprint excerpts from previously published materials.

Harcourt Brace Jovanovich, Inc.: *The Wisdom of the Sands*, by Antoine de Saint-Exupéry,
copyright 1950, 1978, by Harcourt Brace Jovanovich, Inc., reprinted with their
permission.

Alfred A. Knopf, Inc.: "Tonio Kröger," by Thomas Mann. Copyright 1936 and renewed
1964 by Alfred A. Knopf, Inc. Reprinted from *Stories of Three Decades,* by Thomas Mann,
translated by H. T. Lowe-Porter, by permission of Alfred A. Knopf, Inc.

Princeton University Press: *The Collected Works in English,* by Paul Valéry, Bollingen
Series XLV. Vol. 4, *Dialogues,* translated by William McCausland Stewart, copyright
1956 by Princeton University Press. Excerpts as requested. Reprinted by permission
of Princeton University Press.

New York Public Library: previously unpublished letter by Lincoln Kirstein, copyright
2003 by the New York Public Library (Astor, Lenox and Tilden Foundations).

The University Press of Florida is the scholarly publishing agency for the State University
System of Florida, comprising Florida A&M University, Florida Atlantic University,
Florida Gulf Coast University, Florida International University, Florida State University,
University of Central Florida, University of Florida, University of North Florida,
University of South Florida, and University of West Florida.

University Press of Florida
15 Northwest 15th Street
Gainesville, FL 32611-2079
http://www.upf.com

For my mother and father

PREFACE TO THE 2003 EDITION

for Anne Freedgood

Twenty-two years ago, when I first signed a contract with Random House for this book—a brief section of the endless scribbling that had become an Anaïs Nin–type addiction—I went directly to George Balanchine's office on the fourth floor of the New York State Theater to inform him that my diary as a dancer in his company, the New York City Ballet, was to be published. I was afraid I would be fired, very afraid. Not because I had written anything shocking or libelous, but because I had written something at all. Dancers didn't write unless they were stars—only then did they have a story worth telling, the story of success.

My diary bore witness to the opposite, far more prevalent scenario: the transient joys—doing thirty-two *fouettés* ending with a double, finding the perfect pair of toe shoes, living in a world saturated with live classical music—and the endless angst of not being a star, of realizing I probably never would be a solo dancer despite having talent, opportunity, and that haunting dark shadow called potential. I felt deeply committed, and yet totally powerless, to actualize my dream—which was never to be a star *per se,* just to be intoxicatingly beautiful as a dancer, for my passion to physically manifest. No small feat, but every dancer's challenge.

I knocked on the door. Standing outside Mr. B.'s office awaiting entrance was like visiting the Vatican awaiting an audience with the Pope. Even worse: Mr. B. knew far more about *pliés* and *tendus,* the language of my destiny. Most girls knocking on his door were asking for parts, not permission to publish. I wouldn't have dared ask for a role. I only wanted to be allowed to explain on a page how much I wanted parts, why I thought I didn't have them, what I might be able to do about getting them, and what I should do if my "potential" failed me. I was doing more pirouettes with my thoughts than with my legs.

He opened the door, greeted me, and gestured for me to come in and sit down. He sat too. All very simple, very humble. I had vowed not to cry no matter how my visit went; I remembered him telling a weeping friend of mine, "Dear, you cannot be hysterical if you want to dance." But I always felt on the edge of hysteria. My whole life felt like the ballet *La Valse:* dancing in tulle on the verge of volcanic eruption.

Mr. B. listened attentively, and when I finished my rehearsed speech he sat back in his chair and asked me one question about my forthcoming book: "Is it about me, dear?"

"Oh, no!" I assured him. I explained that, although he was mentioned a few times, it was mainly about me. He sniffed and looked vaguely amused. I completely missed the irony of telling the great genius that he was only a supporting character in my own dramatic life.

"Fine, dear," he said. "Just give me a copy when it is ready." He then kissed me on the forehead and sent me back to rehearsal.

In early July 1982 my beloved editor, Anne Freedgood, sent me the first two copies of the book. She wrote in her note, "One for you and the other for Mr. B." By now Balanchine was already ill with the Creutzfeldt-Jakob brain disease that would kill him within a year. At the time it remained undiagnosed. No one knew what was wrong with the choreographer who had now cruelly, literally lost his balance. He was staying in Saratoga Springs while we performed at our annual summer home there, but he was too unsteady to come to the theater.

Peter Martins was beginning to oversee some of the day-to-day running of things and was known to visit Balanchine for breakfast early each morning at the farm where he was staying. I gave the second copy of the book to Peter, asked him to give it to Mr. B., and held my breath. For a whole week. Despite already receiving positive notice in various publications, there was only one review that really mattered. Balanchine was not the star character in my story; he was the god of my world.

Peter reported to me for the ensuing several days that every time he arrived at 7:30 for breakfast, Mr. B. was reading my little book. When he finished it, he told Peter, "She will be a great writer one day . . . *if* she wrote it." I had a really good class that day. Really, really good. Not because I would be a "great writer"—that was just more daunting potential to deal with—but because I had, indeed, written it. It had, apparently, exceeded his expectations.

A few days later, while congregating with the other dancers around the daily schedule board backstage after morning company class, I was suddenly targeted by two blue eyes that looked like side-by-side, bottomless pools. It was The Goddess, Suzanne Farrell—the only one who wasn't sweating.

"Is your book available in legitimate bookstores?" she asked me with a mischievous smile. I was speechless; she had never spoken to me before. When I recovered from the shock I murmured, "I believe so." Were there illegitimate bookstores, I wondered?

To my astonishment, a number of my peers in the company pressed surreptitiously scrawled little notes into my hand in the elevator, or explained to me in hushed but relieved tones that I had written their story, their life. They were giving the book to their parents to explain what it was like to dance at NYCB, to persevere despite the ever-present fear of failure. I, in my youthful myopia, had thought that only I was so alone, so inadequate, so brutalized by insecurity, so tormented by my perceived physical imperfections. I found out—to my great surprise and relief—that everyone was! So I joined the human race, or at least the race of thoroughbred Balanchine dancers. It was a gift indeed.

That fall, back in the city, Balanchine was hospitalized near the New York State Theater at St. Roosevelt's Hospital, where he would eventually die. In February 1983, armed with a homemade orange-nut cake soaked in brandy, I set out to visit him. I stood in the doorway of his private room and he looked up from his bed, recognizing me immediately (I didn't know if he would), and without pausing a beat he said, "Are you still with us, dear?"

"Oh, yes," I confirmed. He thought I might have retired from the stage to write, given my recent literary foray. But no, I was still far more interested in the challenge of dancing than that of writing. It was harder.

As I was leaving after my short visit, Mr. B. said to me, "Why don't you write a story about a man and two women, a man and three women, a man and . . ." I have often wondered what he meant. Did he mean himself and his long line of beloved muses? How interesting, I thought—if that was what he meant. It suggested that he was not so concerned with the importance of his ballets as great works of twentieth-century art. His raison d'être was the story of one man's lifelong adoration and fascination with woman. It was as if the ballets were merely the result, the byproduct, of this obsessive love. He was not concerned with making "masterpieces," or with his immortality. He was interested in exploring and recording the beauty and possibilities, both physical and spiritual, of the female sex. This was the last time I saw him alive.

On April 30, 1983, Mr. B. died. It was a Saturday, and we danced two performances as scheduled. Suzanne and Peter danced the second movement adagio of *Symphony in C*. It was a prayer, their prayer, our prayer. Onstage behind them, I understood in a flash why my youthful atheism was forever challenged by my experience on Balanchine's stage. It seemed so appropriate that we were all in Karinska's fluffy white *Symphony in C* tutus, the widowed brides of Balanchine, each and every one of us.

There were several long memorial services held at the Russian Orthodox Church on 93rd Street near Park Avenue. Hundreds of us stood filling the church, the entry, the stairs, and the sidewalk outside, each holding a single white taper. Balanchine's five wives—Tamara Geva, Alexandra Danilova, Vera Zorina, Maria Tallchief, and Tanaquil Le Clercq—were all there, side by side—Galateas all.

Behind the scenes, the clergy was furious that a man of so many wives would be honored and laid to rest in the Orthodox Church. But Father Adrian insisted, and he presided over the ceremonies; he had been to the ballet and understood the religious nature of Balanchine's work. When the protesting priests—who perceived Balanchine only as a man far too interested in women—saw the mammoth crowd who had come to pay homage, spilling out onto the streets, they were astonished. Who was this man? Who, indeed, was this man, this man who called himself (in the words of the Russian poet Vladimir Mayakovsky) "a cloud in trousers"?

In the fall of 1983, four months after Balanchine's death, the company embarked on a six-week European tour to London, Copenhagen, and Paris. It was an amazing experience: the company danced its heart out for our dead maestro and we were received like orphaned aristocrats. In London we all got sick with the flu, but kept on dancing, of course. One week after arriving in Copenhagen I stepped into line with the rest of the walking wounded, outside our physical therapist's always crowded office. I told Marika Molnar, the therapist, that I couldn't lift my right leg, couldn't walk up the stairs, and definitely couldn't do the opening side kick in *Serenade* that evening. I couldn't dance for the rest of the tour; I could barely walk.

Once back in New York I had a hip X-ray and was called into the office of Dr. William Hamilton, our company orthopedist. "Sit down," he advised—never a good beginning with a doctor. I had developed osteoarthritis in my right hip socket with attendant calcium deposits that left my socket looking craggy as Mount Rushmore when it should be smooth as a Michelangelo marble. He suggested that my career was finished, and that I should stay sitting down. As I gazed at the eerie black and white shadows of bone and missing cartilage in my X-rays, I felt like Hans Castorp in *The Magic Mountain*, looking into my own grave.

I spent several months in bed recovering from the initial

inflammation and then another eight or so months learning to stand in first position all over again. I wasn't succumbing to a doctor's orders. I was omnipotent; I was a Balanchine dancer. A year later I made it back on stage. With my career in the balance, I had finally mastered the art of dancing with a fire under my feet. Assisted by anti-inflammatory drugs, I danced for over a year until compensatory injuries and increasingly alarming X-rays finally forced the truth upon me. I knew that I did not want to martyr myself to my toe shoes. So I retired at the age of twenty-eight.

I have come to think of my hip injury as my war wound in my battle for Beauty, the inevitable scar of so much hard physical work for twenty-five years. And Fate's way of turning my focus from the stage to the page.

My experience in Balanchine's world had given me something worth writing about—the often overlooked, and vastly underrated, imperative for a self-obsessed young writer. I found writing to be the only way to clarify my contradictory feelings and experience internal freedom. The formation of words into comprehensible phrases was my way to be private, publicly, to be a controlled exhibitionist—something I felt I never quite mastered as a dancer.

When I arrived back in New York from Saratoga Springs the summer this book was first published, I found amongst my pile of mail an elegant cream-colored envelope with an engraved return address on the back: "128 East 19th Street, New York City 3." There was no name—but I knew the address. It was a letter from Lincoln Kirstein, with whom I had never spoken. He was the visionary American who in 1933 had invited Balanchine to America. Together they had founded the New York City Ballet. Holding the unopened letter in my hand, I had a sudden and powerful flashback to my days as a student at the School of American Ballet.

Kirstein would visit SAB almost daily. He had an office there, but mostly I think he came to make sure all was going according to the plan, the military-style plan of the school he and Balanchine had established in 1934. The heavy double doors would suddenly swing open, and a cool breeze would blow down the hallway filled with little dancing girls and boys lingering, stretching, complaining, fixing their hair, gossiping, looking like a modern-day version of a Degas painting. All heads would turn in unison as we looked up, way up—Kirstein was huge: six feet two, broad-chested, hawk-like head. All chattering would cease instantly and we would scatter toward the walls, bodies parting like the Red Sea for Moses. Kirstein would barrel straight through the newly formed pathway, lined with young hopefuls. He appeared to look at nothing but saw everything. No one ever dared speak to him. We knew his rules of behavior: (1) there is no justice; (2) it's not fair; (3) be quiet. This was not a democracy; this was a miracle, an aristocracy right in the middle of New York City's upper West Side.

To us young dancers, Kirstein, dressed in his uniform—double-breasted, black Savile Row suit and black Reebok sneakers—was the Darth Vader of the dance world: ominous, impenetrable, daunting, all-powerful. He was also the reason we were there, the reason ballet existed as an American art form.

Only much later did I realize that he was more like Saint Peter guarding the Pearly Gates to the hallowed halls of Balanchine's cathedral.

I opened the letter carefully, trembling. Perhaps now I was to be fired or chastised for going public with my backstage life.

July 29, 1982

Dear Toni Bentley:

I don't think we have ever met, but, having read "Winter Season", I feel I have known you for a long time.

You have written the best book on our company, and have painted the best portrait of Balanchine that exists. Whatever you feel about your present life, it must be some satisfaction to know that, in the future, you will be quoted, and your observation will have the value of a testamentary document.

It is not often that a dancer, as a crafts-master, has won over two languages, steps and words.

Sometime, think of yourself as part of the company's future; not just a corps' dancer, but something on the order of a ballet-mistress. We are in for a period of transition; it is like fifty years ago when we were starting, but now the scale is larger, but the difficulties are equally problematical.

Your intelligence and experience fit you for some sort of future connection; *what* I don't know and have no right to predict, but what you have written earns you a place in our continuous destiny, should you wish to belong to it.

Your career makes you part of a bridge over two periods. You have had some contact with the best of times of the company Balanchine founded; the next five years will be quite different. *Now* is the religion I believe in; steps are in the present, and nostalgia is pure vanity.

I feel you can be of help in securing a new nowness. You have been blessed, or cursed with the unique gift of an awareness of self, which means consciousness as an alternative to mere "happiness". When I pray for the "Lamb of God, take away the sins of the world", I think of our dancers as Lambs of God. Balanchine has a sacral function, and those who are magnetized by his service to God, are indeed blessed. The religious service that the dancers do, is what makes ballet today a replacement of the rituals of organized religion. That is why Suzanne is a very great artist, and why the prayer in "Mozartiana" affects audiences who have no superficial realization of how its steps are combined. Faithfully,

Lincoln Kirstein

This is the most beautiful, most important letter I have ever received. While Kirstein's approval was gratifying, this was not what moved me. He had put my young life into context for me for the first time, and I was able to really grasp that I was part of something greater than my own self.

So how did things end up for the anxious, ambitious young dancer who was me? Spring followed her winter season and with the delivery of Kirstein's letter she experienced a moment of peace, knowing that it had all been worthwhile, that her greatest fear was unfounded and her life did have some meaning. I breathed for the first time in years. I had confessed and been forgiven. Absolution. It is all one can ask for, and more than I ever expected.

Toni Bentley
Los Angeles, 2003

WINTER
SEASON

There are girls who do not like real life. When they hear the sharp belches of its engines approaching along the straight road that leads from childhood, through adolescence, to adultery, they dart into a side turning. When they take their hands away from their eyes, they find themselves in the gallery of the ballet. There they sit for many years feeding their imagination on those fitful glimpses of a dancer's hand or foot. When I was young I too "adored" the ballet. What appeals to these girls is the moonlit atmosphere of love and death.

—*Quentin Crisp,* The Naked Civil Servant

PROLOGUE:
OCTOBER 1969

Her mother went with her. Or perhaps her mother took her. As they walked down the hall, all the studios looked brand-new with bright, glaring lights, big windows, huge mirrors, shiny wood, glowing linoleum. There were girls everywhere; big, tall, thin girls with pretty, powdered, smiling faces. She had never seen so many girls, and she had never seen such old dancers. She had thought only little girls danced.

She changed into her carefully chosen outfit and emerged from the dressing room. Her mother pointed and poked at the lumps and bumps protruding from her tummy. How embarrassing! It was the tunic pants under her leotard—for modesty. They were definitely defeating their purpose.

There was a beautiful girl sitting nearby who looked up and smiled at her. "Don't worry," she said encouragingly, "you'll get in. You have long legs."

She was ushered into the biggest studio along with a few other girls and boys. A round Russian lady began giving a barre. The children stood, one hand gripping the wooden pole, trying their very best to understand and do what was asked for. Strangely, there was no music.

They worked their way through a brief set of exercises. The Russian community—there was a whole clan of foreign-speaking women—stood at the front of the studio taking notes, talking together, challenging one another. They pointed fingers, pronounced names and shook their heads, all the while scribbling on their sheets of paper.

Suddenly they started for her. The whole congregation marched straight at her. Her leg was lifted—to the front, the side, the back, higher and higher it went. The Russian eyebrows rose proportionately. The ladies seemed to agree on something for the first time. The papers were marked.

The children were called into the center of the room to execute an adagio, a pirouette, a pas de basque, a pas de bourrée—the basic steps. Then they were asked to do a big jump—a tour jeté. Her moment arrived. She was the only child who knew it. She could not fail.

The audition was over. The tense, tired children filed out of the studio into the dressing room and emerged to sit quietly beside their accompanying adults. One by one, names were called. The results were read. Sad and tearful faces emerged from the tiny office. Finally her name was called. She marched with her mother into the office. Yes, she was lovely; yes, they would take her; yes, she was thin, graceful and lovely. She would begin classes tomorrow. She would be in the fifth division and wear a shocking-pink leotard. She would take five classes a week.

She was thrilled, thrilled by a success that she had not planned. In fact, until the moment she realized that she had been singled out from the other children, she had never before known the feeling of success. It was a happy feeling. She also realized somewhere below the surface that her success was inevitably connected with the failure of others.

And so she began, eleven years old and with her first taste of success. It was hard for her. It was all so new. All those other girls, so thin, so strong, so good, so pretty, knew more steps than she did.

Five months later, there was a phone call to her home. They were not so sure about her. They weren't sure about her talent or her future—or her feet. Her feet were not strong enough; they did not arch enough. They were not sure she could continue after this year.

She was angry. Very angry. She threw her beloved toe shoes down the incinerator. Her parents were shocked at the apparent pain she felt.

In time she calmed down and continued. But she was different now. The shock had inspired her. She was determined that she would not fail.

She remained at the school for seven years and moved from the bottom of the class to the top. By her last year she was the only one left from her original class. All the rest had been weeded out. They had either grown too tall or fallen in love or gone to college.

During her last year she injured her foot. It was her first injury, and it was more than a coincidence that it came at such a crucial point in her career. She could not dance for three months. The day she returned to class, George Balanchine, the director of the school and of the New York City Ballet, came to watch. He was choosing the girls who would dance the ballerina parts in the school's workshop performance. This performance would be the deciding factor in these young girls' careers.

She was chosen along with two other girls to learn Princess Aurora in *The Sleeping Beauty*.

Rehearsals lasted six months. The week before the performance she slipped—she came down badly from a pas de chat. She saw her performance, her Princess and her career disappear before her eyes. Her ankle turned black and blue and swelled. She sat for the last week of rehearsals in a chair, her foot packed in ice. On the morning of the performance, she got up and danced. She felt no pain at all. She was injured for a month afterwards. But she had danced, and she had triumphed. She was not going to give up the chance of a lifetime.

INTRODUCTION

I am a dancer in the New York City Ballet. I wrote the pages that follow during one ballet season. I began on November 21, 1980, and finished on February 15, 1981. I was lonely; I was sad. I had decided to be alone, but I had never decided to be lonely. I started writing on a yellow pad. I wrote, and I smoked. Every page was covered with a film of smoke.

My dancing was not going well, and I had ambition. I had always had ambition, at least ever since they told me my first year in the school that I might not make it. I did not know what "it" was. But if I could not have it, it was definitely what I wanted. It was the first thing I had ever wanted.

I took my first ballet lesson at the age of three. My mother thought that it would give her skinny little girl an appetite and some grace. We did not live in New York City then, and I was not a driven child. I allowed myself to be led once a week to this very casual affair. When I was ten, we moved to the city, and new schools had to be arranged. I came to the School of American Ballet almost by chance. Somewhere my mother heard of this dancing school—in the elevator, at the laundromat or from a friend of a friend. I auditioned. Neither my mother nor I had the slightest idea of the possible consequences this audition might have. What made me successful that day was not the will to dance, only the desire to please. But I was accepted, and my life changed.

I found myself committed to an extremely competitive environment of beautiful young women. By the time I was thirteen I had ballet classes at ten-thirty each morning and at two-thirty and five-thirty each afternoon. To accommodate this full-time schedule I attended the Professional Children's School, which was dedicated to squeezing a little science, mathematics and English literature into very busy children—musicians, actors, skaters, models and dancers. I had an English class from eight-fifteen to ten each morning, rushed over to Lincoln Center for ballet class and then rushed back to eat my lunch in biology class. I had a home-packed lunch which was always the same: three medium-sized sandwiches filled with leftovers from dinner the night before, a bag of Fritos, an apple and two Hostess Twinkies. Most days I would refuse to share any of it. I was growing a lot. PCS was very hectic and very amusing. And very secondary in importance.

Seven years later I made it. I was chosen by Mr. Balanchine. I joined the company.

That was a great day, the day that my future was decided. I probably had an ice cream. If I didn't, I should have. I remember saying to myself, praying to myself, "If I can only get in, I'll be happy, I'll be satisfied. I'll never ask for more." I did not realize what a deeply sad day it actually was—the end of a dream and the beginning of reality.

I not only got in, I was chosen to learn things. Big, grand ballerina things. Pink things—I was definitely the pink type. I still am, but I am surprised that it showed way back then. I had not yet learned what it meant. Sometimes I think that pink is my fate. They are forever trying to replace people. Replace Patricia McBride or Suzanne Farrell? But they keep trying.

And so one month after achieving my dream, I was handed another. Only I was not told that this one was improbable. That could have been the problem. I was warned of nothing. I was not told they were checking out potential. Maybe it is always like that. Youth is always regarded as potential. And while they are waiting and watching one's potential, one is surprisingly alive.

I kept on doing my tendus, and my ambition was very well fed. Ambition is always well fed in the New York City Ballet. That is why we are so good. Then one day my ambition was put on a diet, just like the rest of me. My name was seen with others. It had been seen alone. So perhaps the road to Ballerina Land was not going to be as straight as I had planned. In fact, I got the strange feeling that I wasn't even doing the planning anymore. It was devastating.

The straight lines started zigzagging. They zigzagged all over the place. Going forward used to mean going forward. I think now that it means going backward. And then something happened: life. I had had no impositions from this culprit. I was not stupid. When he beckoned to me, I laughed and said no. I didn't want life. I wanted to dance. But he persisted. He can be pretty persuasive. I would even say that he gave me no choice.

Maybe I can't say that. This particular form of life is quite well known, at least in the ballet world. It is known to be dangerous. I was well prepared, but he had deep blue eyes. I was moved by this form of life, but it was the wrong form. And so I started zigzagging.

I still have a dream. I dream of finding a straight line. I think that it is a good dream, for I will never realize it; it will last forever. Nevertheless, I tried to achieve this dream by returning to the actions that had accompanied my first dream. They had succeeded. And so from November 21, 1980, to February 15, 1981, I was busy. I worked. I smoked. And I wrote. This is what I wrote.

. . . and the dancers showed their activity before the princes, in hope that they should pass their lives in this blissful captivity, to which those only were admitted whose performance was thought able to add novelty to luxury. . . . Thus every year produced new schemes of delight and new competitors for imprisonment.

—*Samuel Johnson,* The History of Rasselas, Prince of Abyssinia

November 21, 1980: It is 10:45, performance is over, and I feel I must now begin to write. A dancer is like any artist, his art is his communication. But tonight I looked out there and felt no rapport at all with those three thousand faces. I know they are all just like Mom and Dad, but it's no good —I perform so much better in rehearsal for my fellow dancers and the one or two faces standing up front. I need the closeness of another, I guess. I don't believe that each face out there has a mind all its own that can really see and feel me. The result of this lack of communication: I become a body in motion without meaning for the audience and, worst of all, devoid of any meaning because I have no meaning for myself. I am somehow unable to capture belief in myself. I feel that without a specific reaction, I make no impression. And if we get no reaction, we all feel rather nonexistent, don't we?

I am a success. I am in the New York City Ballet. But how sad that I must tell myself desperately each day that this is indeed a wonderful thing. I live twenty-four hours a day, twelve inside the theater in a magnificently artistic, creative world. A world that has created that predisposition in me—to be creative. Dancing is an education in the life conducive to creativity. This I've absorbed since I was eleven. Now that I'm twenty-two, I have all the background and discipline to be creative, and dancing is not serving my purpose at all. Unless you're out there on the big stage *alone,* you've no chance to communicate and know you're being successful.

Everyone knows that I've been sad for a few days. I used to hide behind wide smiles of glee, but now that I'm strong enough to be sad, I let it show more—or perhaps I've no strength, no time for masks anymore. And what a show of sympathy I receive! Misery loves company: others' sadnesses feed off mine tonight. How cheerful all my dressing-room pals seemed, and how deeply they searched and questioned my passive face with maternal sympathy: "Well, how was

Goldberg? I really think you should tell Jerry Robbins that you don't want to do that dance."

I just finished *Goldberg Variations*—it was horrible. I felt before each entrance that I could not do it. The moment I set foot on stage, it wasn't me. I charge to the dressing room, look at my face in the mirror under a cloud of cigarette smoke. My makeup is beautiful; my hair is divine; I look great, even magnificent. But out there I was numb. Looking in the mirror re-establishes me; then the thoughts flow into a barrage of hatred for mirrors, our obsession. I dance far better for myself in front of a mirror. At least then I know I have a receptive audience. Oh dear, this is not good dancing, I'm definitely missing the point. I have prepared myself to be beautiful and to be chosen for that beauty. But I feel unchosen.

I think too much, far too much, to dance. For years I've been told this by friends, lovers, teachers and messiahs. Maybe I should have listened and stopped thinking. But must thinking be the death of my career? Is it something to do with spontaneity and momentary living? He who thinks is on the road to wondering why he is alive, which leads to the fact that he is indeed alive—which means he will die. We dancers have no thought of death; we can't. We can't even think of the future, because we have no future: no financial security, no education for any other profession. Balanchine says, *"Now, now*—what are you waiting for?" This requires not only *no* thinking but a rejection of thinking. "Don't worry, just do." "Don't think, just do." But I keep on thinking.

I guess I'm trying to find a worthy excuse for my current failure in dancing. But that was not what I set out to do. I want to describe my life. I want to create something out of my life, on paper if I can't on stage.

Funny how I adore all those lovely "pretty things" called dancers, whose bodies and faces are so sculpted and graceful, but the fact that I am such a creature means nothing to me.

DANCERS

We are hairless. We have no leg hairs, no pubic hair, no armpit hair, no facial hair, no neck hair and only a solid little lump at the top of our heads. Any sign of stubble must be closely watched out for and removed.

That is not all. We don't eat food, we eat music. We need artistic sustenance only. Emotional, inspiring sustenance. All our physical energy is the overflow of spiritual feelings. We live on faith, belief, love, inspiration, vitamins and Tab.

We live only to dance. If living were not an essential prerequisite, we would abstain.

We have a different bodily structure than most humans. Our spirits, our souls, our love reside totally in our bodies, in our toes and knees and hips and vertebrae and necks and elbows and fingertips. Our faces are painted on. We draw black lines for eyes, red circles for cheekbones and ovals for a mouth.

Any hint of facial wrinkles, teary eyes, drops of sweat, audible breathing or diminishing energy levels is a sign of imperfection. They are symptoms of mortality.

You know, you wake up and look out the window. It's beautiful and sunny. Then you have a bad class, and the day is ruined.

I share a dressing room with seven other girls who are of the older generation. They've almost reached adulthood. One girl is sprawled on the bed. Another is taking off her pointe shoes: "First I rub this aspirin ointment on my foot—I guess it's absorbed through the skin. Then I put Saran Wrap around it, then an Ace bandage, then a sock and a heating pad —all night. Otherwise I can't plié when I wake up."

Our first thought on waking up is, can I plié? Imagine a mathematician who could not think in formulas when he awoke unless he had had a cigar and four ounces of green grapes the night before! We have certain recipes for working. They are physical because unfortunately our poor old muscles are not as reliable as our poor old minds. They must be treated like babies—rests, Jacuzzi baths, ice packs, bandages, Epsom salts, creams and God knows what else!

Another thing about us—with our heads full of toe shoes, ribbons, and soaking our feet—is that we find it difficult to socialize with "normal" people. They are curious, starstruck, charmed by us, and totally frustrated when they can find no points of common interest. Books and politics are definitely out; TV and movies maybe. But worse than that, when it comes to sheer living, well, we simply must go to bed, and it is far better not to be full of Scorpions from Trader Vic's!

One gives in to the temptation a few times, but the side effects are just not worth the fun. Our spontaneity is on stage, not in late-night revelry. But how we love to hear of one another's straying from the path! All ears are pricked when the story of a crazed evening on the town is described. The younger ones especially listen in awe and innocence. Such living is as alien and confusing to us as dancing every day would be to most people. Yes, we are definitely curious creatures. And in moments of weakness we try to reassure ourselves that it is worth it, and best of all, that one has the whole rest of one's life to live. We call "living" what we don't do—we dance, we don't live. After all, we are allowed none of the decorations—no love life, no food, no liquor, no late nights, no drugs. This is the general rule. Of course we all are human and forget ourselves periodically and lapse into "living" habits, but the inevitable repercussions always let us know when living is interfering with dancing!

About money: I really think we are the most ignorant paid people on earth. I'm sure we are constantly cheated and never complain. We are not trained to think financially. Money is only to pay for the apartment, to buy a fur coat and ballet clothes. I often save money, but it is purely by mistake. We live as we must dance—now. When we have a need, we write a check. It's the only way we know. All our excess money goes on clothes and bodily adornments. We live to adorn ourselves.

I sometimes worry that when I stop dancing and start living, my incredible consciousness of physical beauty is going to be a real problem. Especially with men. I thought a giant step had been taken when I found a big round tummy not only not disagreeable but quite lovely and cuddly. I thought to myself, I can grow to love normal people. A few years ago I was convinced beyond a doubt that I could never ever love a man who had flat feet. Feet were incredibly important to me. And as for having no calves or muscle tone— well, I still have my doubts. But by mistake, I liked a man who did have flat feet. I liked him first, then noticed his feet —and then, thank God, it was too late to say no! I suppose everyone has prejudices, and ours are physical. We can't help it; the first things we notice are bodies.

I don't think that there is any dancer who does not harbor this dream of the future: to eat three meals a day—French toast with butter and syrup, ice cream sodas and three-course dinners with wine—and not to have to grab a yogurt or coleslaw in a half-hour break for dinner. On the other hand, our minds and hearts are focused on other, far more important things—a flat tummy, warming up, makeup, and the endless toe-shoe sewing. Food is unnecessary.

We really are a funny class of society—we come from all backgrounds, from mailmen's kids to doctors' and lawyers' kids. We are uneducated, apolitical and generally amoral—except where dancing is concerned. Because dancing is now at such a peak of popularity, we are accepted by the world as desirable social beings, but we are really pretty alien. We are always performing, even on social occasions—playing the role of the dancer. We don't know what else to be. A famous male dancer said to me recently, "I don't know how to live. I've no house, no home. I can't do anything but point my toes and stage ballets." He said he thinks he'll die early, before he has to cope with living. But he wasn't sad when he said it, only melodramatic, pleased with his role of the dancer who cannot live.

Perhaps the best dancers are like this. Some do know how to live and try desperately to find the time to do so. You can pick them out at a glance: they have this conflict, this struggle, this torture on their faces every time they take a step. It's as if every step on the stage is a step away from any other kind of existence that they know and love. Each drop of sweat deepens one's dedication and takes one further from real life. Dancing is a commitment that refutes real life. A dancer told me, "Well, it's only dancing. It's only dancing; then there is life." That dancer has a life, a private life; he is a wonderful chef, collects paintings and has outside friends. You can see it on his face when he dances.

We are basically very honest people. You might say it has something to do with being artists. We are unable to cheat ourselves. We know what is true and what is not. Art rests on sincerity, of course, but I think it is simpler than that: we are naive, innocent in the ways of the world; after all, we grew up in ballet school. I've been out with rich businessmen who gladly accept my half of the bill when I offer to pay it—and I gladly offer, telling myself that I'm contributing to his future financial security. I know I myself have none!

I once heard a principal dancer say, "I do my best, and now I'm trying to learn to enjoy it." It struck me that the enjoyment comes last: first one does the work, then one tries to have a good time. I dance best when I have joy already and I dance to celebrate it. It's difficult, dancing, when the aim is to express beauty and joy, and the means to do it is work. The work must give the joy that must be the result. It's a vicious cycle. I think the joy misses out a lot.

November 22: I just had an uneventful *Stars and Stripes* rehearsal. I also just got about a hundred dollars for chiffon skirts. I sew, and the others buy—most satisfying!

On second thought, rehearsal was uneventful in terms of the ballet, but as with everything, it was very eventful internally. Every time Rosemary, our ballet mistress, stopped to correct someone, I thought, Jesus, it's me, what did I do? and then sighed with relief when she accused the girl next to me. No doubt all twelve girls were thinking the same. And there was the usual response: "Yes, I have it up here [a finger to the head] but not down here [a finger to the feet]." We have that problem a lot. Instant corrections are rare; some of us are better at it than others. We call them good learners, those who are instantly physical; they have brains in their toes, I guess. Like baby birds, they see it and do it, whereas some of us see it, filter it through our heads and then reapply it to our bodies—a process that definitely wastes time!

Sometimes we blow soap bubbles in the dressing room. It was my idea. We laugh at them and make up stories about them.

Every season when we move into our dressing room we have a refrigerator problem. Last season we thought we'd have to get a new one. The door was off altogether and used to drop with a crash at the appropriate crescendo of the music. (The performance is played over the loudspeakers all the time so we know which ballet is going on.) But some of the stagehands fixed it. Then there is the mold. No one wants to clean out the goddamned mold, so for a while we carefully wrapped our food up and deposited it in the mold. Finally one of us got so disgusted she cleaned it, and we never heard the end of the gruesome details and her sacrifice.

Heather Watts just executed her first *Theme and Variations* in New York. She danced it once in Paris. I watched from my prime spot in the second wing. She was not lovely— not soft—but quite, quite great. The ballerina of ballerina parts, she is out there crowning all, and I don't think it would be amiss to say her dream has come true. She dances with the desire and guts and intensity of that dream. It is romantic, what she has done, like it or not. It makes me feel rather feeble when I think I want and desire things. I've never desired as she desires. I probably can't and never will —few of us could. She knew what she wanted and went for it straight as an arrow. I admire that and feel very, very feeble right now, having witnessed her success.

Mr. B. stood in his front wing for *Theme*. His latest attire: glasses, one without any glass and one black. I doubt if he'd mind if I say he looked very evil, like a pirate, Errol Flynn style. Afterwards he had words of advice. He objected strongly to the boys' hair hanging in their faces: "It looks like you're coming from the toilet"—he always has such a way with words.

As I left the theater, I detected an all-too-familiar hand-writing on a scrawled note to another girl from an ex-boyfriend of mine. I grinned. Was I defensive? I doubt it.

About the dance, tonight maybe I enjoyed being an audience more than being a performer. It is so easy to identify with all that greatness and wonder going on out there while feeling very comfortable. Rather a cop-out, really. Being out on the gangplank alone is left to those few who dare; we all sit and watch. I rather detest that in myself.

I'll say no more tonight. I feel too serious and humble. I think I'd better start some lists for Christmas or something.

I have this late-night vice. I scratch my toes ferociously. They itch so much, I can never help thinking that there is something of deep significance in this painful cycle of masochism. It doesn't help in pointe shoes the next morning.

"Our lives revolve around what we don't eat."

Everyone always wonders what dancers eat to stay so slim. Well, to each his own. I know what I eat—and very strangely, too, very consciously, savoring every mouthful: eggs, bran muffins, salads, melon, ice cream, fish—real-people food. I think the strangeness comes in how we eat and when. Never at mealtimes. The only possible real meal is after performance at eleven o'clock, and then you're up all night. We tend to pick at dishes smorgasbord-style so as not to miss a thing but not to finish anything. There is surprising psychological satisfaction in just a bite or two of something. Quality not quantity in food is a distinction well made. But we love cakes, ice cream, fudge, chocolate doughnuts. If any are around, they are breathed in. I guess we all eventually find the weight and "look" we like and know what food suffices for it. But we have a lot of faddy ideas: "Sugar freaks me out"; "Take B_{12}, really, B_{12} will fix everything"; and on it goes.

I think I reveal no great secrets by saying that Heather Watts is associated with junk food, Mr. Balanchine and Suzanne Farrell with gourmet food, Kyra Nichols and Dan Duell with hamburgers and Alexia Hess with anything. Oh yes, Gerry Ebitz with peanut butter and jelly on Wonder Bread.

Smoking? We shouldn't, but we do—a great deal less than other companies, however. It is not approved of.

We adore a good party after the performance, especially on tour. We are very, very good at generating party spirits. It makes perfect sense—the extremes of classic discipline and outrageous wacky behavior.

Our hosts love us at parties—glamorous, beautiful and wild, with a bizarre sense of humor. That's because it's all physical, our humor, I mean, parodies of ballets and music, that sort of thing. At parties we can perform without having to stay in line; it's delightful. It reminds me of airports—NYCB roaming Kennedy departure terminal. We torment the people in restaurants and bookshops with our demands. What can they expect when the public is such an instant audience? Everyone is all eyes and ears, so we react. We are funny, wild—and vulgar, I suppose.

Once we are on the plane, I look down the aisle and see a hundred dancers standing, moving, smoking, talking, gesticulating. Legs are stretched and posed and propped up—on display. The colors are bright and mixed: gold threads, gold sparkles, gold socks, gold jewels, gold hair clips, purples, pinks, reds, greens, blues, whites. There are hats and feathers, belts and bags, magazines, books and Walkman radios.

No one does anything for long. We prance and dance and

dip and sway. We change seats, we change occupations, we change clothes. We are a haphazard lot, seemingly undirected but not really, not really at all. We are dedicated to a 100 percent physical-energy output, and today's allotment is as yet unused.

November 23: We just had a hilarious time in *Rubies* as a new girl happily jogged all around the stage sixteen counts early while the rest of us stood stationary. She looked like an escaped jumping bean.

We are discussing our new contract, and, typically, very few of us are interested in such things as raises and union rules, but tomorrow there is a promise of fudge and brownies at the meeting, so I predict a large turnout. The prospect of sugar holds greater allure for us than a hundred-dollar-a-week pay raise. Aren't we unique?

I just want to put in something here about Suzanne— Suzanne Farrell. Not a review but an adoration. In *Diamonds* tonight she glowed as no diamond ever could. I love her, I want to say that, I want everyone to know that. My life would be different without her. She has changed my life, that's all. And she can be so wonderfully funny. Upon being complimented for a performance of *Diamonds* she smiled and said, "The lights were so bright, couldn't you tell I was looking down more than usual?" "No." "Then it works to paint eyeballs on your eyelids."

To long to be allowed to live the life of simple feeling, to rest sweetly and passively in feeling alone, without compulsion to act and achieve—and yet to be forced to dance, dance the cruel and perilous sword-dance of art; without even being allowed to forget the melancholy conflict within oneself; to be forced to dance, the while one loved.

— *Thomas Mann*, "Tonio Kröger"

I think I'd like to write the next part as fiction.

There was once a young dancer—very young. I know all stories begin this way, but so do all dancers. She had just been accepted in a wonderful big famous ballet company. She had just successfully danced the ballerina role in her school performance, and her school work was finishing. She was all toe shoes, pink chiffon, hard work and wide eyes. Life was just beginning, every day new thrills—free toe shoes, a paycheck, new ballets to learn and some very special ballets. She had been singled out to understudy one of the leading ballerinas in several parts.

Every day was busy and miraculous, and her ambition knew no bounds. Oh yes, she lived with her parents still— this is important later. She had very wonderful parents. And they could not have been more pleased; there was their young daughter already professional at her chosen trade.

And so her whole life was dancing. She had done well at academic school, but predictably she dropped all her books as soon as it was allowed. As for the opposite sex—

well, she knew it existed, and that was quite enough. She had read the facts but retained no personal interest; that was for other, older people. Sex was foreign country, and she preferred staying on home ground. To be sure, she had played around with her little girl friends, but no curiosity had come of it. Oh yes, I almost forgot, she had gone to an X-rated movie once with a friend. In it the woman had given herself pleasure. That was undeniably an area of unexplored curiosity for a young narcissistic dancer. It also had occurred to our young heroine, let us call her Isabelle, that this had not been just acting. And in very little time Isabelle found her "acting" quite up to that of the film's actress. But this remained a very private matter; Isabelle was a dancer in all her priorities.

Isabelle was as innocent as the princess in a fairy tale. Then one night she was kissed by a boy. That really decided matters; she wanted to dance. So now you see Isabelle, young, pretty and dedicated. And then you see a big star— a big ballet superstar, a handsome male superstar. Very handsome. Handsome in that awesome, evil way. He did not look innocent. He was famous for his evil aura. Without really trying, he was magnetic to both his audience and his peers. Many moons later Isabelle could not help wondering about this strange attraction. Was it so powerful because it was evil, or was it evil for any man to wield such power? She never got far in her musings, for she always hit the same impasse—it came from the gut, something deeply, fantastically and terrifyingly physical. Animal, or how else could she reconcile the undeniable appeal that even invincible little she succumbed to.

That night she had been thrown into a new ballet, a special part. She was terribly nervous—everyone was there to see her—and she messed up royally. Seventeen girls hopped out, and Isabelle hopped in, straight in. Oh God, it was awful. She was convulsed with tears and wanted to hide, but she had to dance in the last ballet, so she pulled herself together.

Now let's put her in the third wing watching the second ballet. She is alone and in the last stages of composing herself. Well, the superstar, let's call him the Duke, walks up behind her—what nerve, she thought later—and asks how her new part went. She was astonished that he even knew about her or her new part. Honest and innocent as she was, she confessed her disaster, but he thought that it didn't matter. He asked her out after performance; they were both in the last ballet. "Absolutely not. I know what you want." She was insulted to be approached by a man of such ill repute. I doubt personally that she could have looked at him, because I certainly could not have refused those blue eyes. But he was adorably insistent, and when he asked that the invitation be kept a secret, she relented. Yes, she thought, my own private little episode. That appealed to her private little ballerina self.

The Duke was the star of the last ballet. As Isabelle stood in the corps behind him, watching those huge muscles flex and release to the wild screams of the audience, she could hardly contain herself. Just think, she thought, three thousand people want him now, and in ten minutes he'll be with little old me.

And so they went out. He ate a steak while she watched, sipping white wine (she was still at the stage of her career of not eating, maintaining her self-control, and she was magnificent at it). Since she was not eating, she talked, on and on and on. She had a grand time showing the star herself. No doubt he did everything appropriate; he was a charmer, after all. But after dinner, home on the bus to Mom and Dad she went. Quite exciting—the Duke had been hers for an evening, and that was enough for her.

I just thought a funny thought. This is only a story, but I can imagine protests. After all, how many such Dukes and such episodes have occurred in the wings of every ballet company around the world? I might get some interesting mail—everyone claiming to be the Duke of my story!

"All of her was love! And that is why only a dancer can make it visible by the beauty of her actions."

—*Paul Valéry,* Dance and the Soul

November 25: I am repeating myself, but I must. Suzanne just finished another *Diamonds,* and frankly I cannot put any words on paper to describe her magnificence, her giving. I watch her face and can only think of a love she has greater than I could ever contain. She is from God's world—a direct disciple, I think. He has sent her down to brighten our lives and teach us of higher things. To me she is beauty itself—the word came after her presence. Each time she smiles, I can only cry, and I think of something I read about the sadness of beauty: just to find it is not so hard, but to bear it, that is impossible. If Suzanne were totally aware of the beauty she was creating, she would stop in awe of herself. She somehow makes life so much more than it is and then—well, I am absolutely at a loss.

I suppose the first reaction to such a sight and emotion is to define it. Isn't that what critics do? By defining and trying to explain her we attempt, I'm sure, to submerge and put aside the sadness that her simple self evokes. She is not to be explained—she cannot be—but it is hard to bear such a sight. Surely any of our mortal words put down to explain her or describe her are absurd. She is, that is all; but how can we learn to bear it? Each time I finish *Rubies* and know that *Diamonds* is to follow, I wonder whether to subject myself to her or to carry on my own little life in my own little world and do otherwise. But somehow I go back again and again for more—more and more sadness.

Someone pointed out to me the other day the incredible diamond décolleté of her costume—so many flashing rhinestones, they are blinding. I had never noticed. Her face, her smile, her eyes distract from the sparkle of her costume.

There is a strange irony in our hierarchical situation. When one is first a member of the company, one dances every ballet. Then as one proceeds, one is taken out of ballets and the younger kids move in. It is a point of great triumph and a sign of seniority to be "out" of a ballet. To dance less is a sign of great respect. Rather strange when the object is to dance, but so it goes. On the same premise, to be left in *Swan Lake* past one's peers is a sign, a warning that things are not so good. The complaints about still being in *Swan Lake* are numerous and never-ending. People demand to be out of ballets, and then of course complain because they don't dance. It's rather like everything in life—the grass is always greener elsewhere.

Our schedule for each day is mapped out for us only the evening before. Usually by eight o'clock, curtain time, a pencil-written schedule is posted on the bulletin board at stage level. A crowd immediately gathers for a quick silent perusal before stepping on stage. During the performance, things are canceled, added or rearranged, according to the casualty level of the performance. If a dancer is injured, the ballet must be re-rehearsed for the understudy, or if the dancer is irreplaceable, a whole new ballet must be rehearsed as a replacement. By eleven P.M., the schedule can be assumed to be final, although in the course of the next day things are often changed.

It begins with the names of the dancers who must visit Madame Karinska, our designer, for costume fittings. Class always comes next at ten-thirty, ten forty-five or eleven. Who is teaching is of the utmost importance. Is it Balanchine? Rehearsals begin at noon and continue until six or later if there are "emergencies."

The schedule is our reference point all day long. It dictates our when, where and what; the why is understood.

The schedule is also taped on a special phone number for those who have the performance off and are not in the theater. Since it contains the first information on casting changes, it is a very nerve-wracking phone call. How often I have called to be thrilled or tearful or suicidal!

Our current contract is up; in fact, it was finished in September, and here we are in November, typically, working without one. I think that is rather rare, but then we dancers are dedicated to the art, not the money.

Quite a lot of company spirit is being aroused, more than ever before. This means that 80 percent of us know that we don't have a contract, and twenty or thirty people out of one hundred show up at union meetings!

Meetings are a curious coming together of two worlds —young dancers and middle-aged, rotund, complacent union people. Our union is the American Guild of Musical Artists—AGMA. We sit on the floor cracking our necks, stretching our toes, braiding our hair, giving massages, chewing gum, drinking soda and smoking. Most faces are blank and only visually follow the conversation. Once in a while, to everyone's delight, someone has an idea to voice, and we are most supportive—to anything that is said. If a dancer speaks, it must have value. What I'm trying to say is that we are all grossly ignorant of money matters, our rights, and even what we can and should demand—but we try. We attempt to explain to these men our perverse and unique situation. We are under the dictatorship of one man, whom we adore and respect, and his every whim is our law, no questions asked.

A union? A democracy under a dictator? We have no power to strike, really. Who would do that to our god? Rather lovely and unique, isn't it? Typically, the meeting was kept alive by sodas, fudge and comic relief—loud cracks, a prance and curtsy across the room. Only then were all the faces alert and comprehending.

I read something in the paper today about a pseudo-science of body knowledge. The idea is that someone who uses his body and muscles learns and retains a superior intuitive knowledge of life that the intellectual, the reader, misses. That's us, all right. We can't always talk, but God knows we know.

November 26: Well, I am not dancing tonight, but I have my self-respect. That's what it has come down to. I refused to replace a girl in what was originally my part; I became "too small" and was taken out. Then they asked me to replace her when she was ill. I refused, so I don't dance but have loads of self-respect. I can envision the day when one has nothing but self-respect. How hideous. But right now I feel good. Even dancers, I suppose, must demand their rights, but they are the ones who lose. Balanchine has said more than once: "We dancers are the only people who can have our cake and eat it too." For four years I've wondered exactly what that means. On occasion it makes sense, but then it is lost again.

November 27: Well, it's Thanksgiving, and I must confess that I have a lot to say but no desire to say it. It's all rather self-contained joy with no frustrated edges. We had the day off but a performance at night; there were endless turkey jokes. We look like turkeys, feel like turkeys, and dance like turkeys. We feel thick, loaded, drunk, heavy and humorous. We decide that we should always have free days and perform only at night, it is so much more fun. Perry Silvey, the stage manager, announces the half-hour with "Good evening, turkeys." There is great family feeling backstage. Warm-ups are minimal, mainly verbal. Stories, jokes— *Goldberg* and *Stars and Stripes*—what a program! First the audience can sleep and then wake up in time to leave. As for us, I overhear a comment: "I didn't think we'd do *Stars* on Thanksgiving again since Hermes threw up." *Stars* is hard.

My thanks today are much in order—my third period in a row. Ah, the joy of a fluid body that eats and drinks and sweats and moves. The monthly flow arrives and explains me to myself—my emotions, my moods, my desires, my softness. I am relieved.

I am questioned doubtfully by my dressing room. "Are you sure you're a dancer?" This is a bad sign, normalcy. Really, it's a first since I was fourteen. Between the strenuous work, the emotional highs and lows, and the starvation level we maintain, periods are indeed a rare occurrence. Anyway, at least last week's suicidal tendencies are well explained!

On the way to the theater I overhear one of those raving street philosophers who proliferate on holidays: "The Jews make believe they're living, the Catholics make believe they're living. Everyone makes believe they're living. The blacks avoid the whites; the whites avoid the blacks. What's it all about?" I did overhear one, only one, dedicated statement tonight: "He tried to make me have a meal, but I'm a dancer; I don't take vacations."

I have just seen the *New York Times* review of *Theme,* the one in which I thought Heather Watts was quite great. Anna Kisselgoff had this to say: "Mr. Martins also partnered Miss Watts in 'Theme and Variations.' Her solos were marred by incomplete movements, but the pas de deux went smoothly, and Mr. Martins was called back for an extra bow after a superbly polished solo."

You know what is hellishly frightening about dancing? One puts all one's energy, time and guts into it, and then it ends each night, and then for good in a few years. Poof, that's it, no more, no lasting effects, no basis has been built, it is just finished.

There are quite a few very frightening stories of dancers who have stopped dancing. They are like lost children: no direction, no knowledge, no goals. They have absolutely nothing with which to confront the world or life. There are some sad stories about years of doing nothing, drugs, illegitimate babies, divorces, breakdowns. Oh, dear dancer, beware of avoiding life now, for sooner or later you will have to face it.

Perhaps in every ballet-school curriculum there should be one hour a week for learning about life, the world and other possibilities. Of course this could never be enforced. Dancers know only one thing, and that is precisely why they can devote themselves to it so totally. They don't give themselves a choice. I've noticed the most dedicated girls tend to be those with ballet-family backgrounds. Born thinking about their toes, they have not strayed from the track since day one.

I've had some more thoughts on our contract business. We are the greatest ballet company in the free world because we live under a total dictatorship. We are all there for one reason and one man—Balanchine is our leader, and we are his subjects. For us to strike for our rights would be going against the only reason we are here at all.

TOE SHOES

They cost $30 a pair ($4 extra because we have them made to order individually) and have to be sent from England, where little old men are sewing day in and day out. We each have a "maker" designated by his mark on the shoe. I have Y, and there is a frightening rumor around that Mr. Y is dying or retiring. Well, we Y devotees are at a real loss. Some of us have already been given P—such messing around with our shoes over in England, where we have no control, is not taken lightly! As a result, I have just changed my shoe order:

Toni Bentley

NYCB	*heel: 2 3/4" long*
6 FBT—*102 5-4m*	*vamps: 3 3/4" long*
6 FBT—*102 5-4x*	*Phillips Insole*
Spade maker- ♠	*Extra paste at tips*
sides: 2" long	*Extra flat platform*

Same specifications for both sizes

We use at least twelve pairs a week, very often more. That's at least $360 per girl per week, times fifty-four girls. That's $19,440 a week times fifteen weeks a season—$291,-600. Very expensive footwear.

We take them out of their plastic bags, pour Fabulon in the toes (to harden them), sew on ribbons and elastic, cut out the satin toe (it's slippery), pull out the insole (it's excess), soak the toes in water or alcohol (they're too hard and too small), step on them (they're too round), bend the shank in half (it's too straight), shave the leather off the bottoms with a rasp (it's too slippery), and bang them on the wall (they're too noisy). We then put them on for a fifteen-minute ballet and as soon as it is over throw them out (there is no life left in them). A very quick $30! But not one of us thinks for a moment about it. To us they are simply toe shoes—essential, but enemies that must be beaten.

Our other dancing clothes, besides our costumes, consist of leotards, tights, leg warmers, socks, sweaters, scarves, tops, sweat pants, sweat shirts, skirts, and every possible variation of these articles. Every color, too, not just black and pink, though these are basic. In fact a bright-red sweat shirt, to the knees of course, is a bold and welcome subject for conversation. We observe, discuss and criticize outfits just as if we were experts at a fashion show, although I imagine we are both more critical and more open-minded. Ideas are stolen daily; our outfits are basic to our thought and work. They are our expression of mood and attitude, and a new one could be the beginning of a great day or a great phase of progress—or regress!

We keep this wardrobe at the theater in our dressing room, on hangers, on the many shelves, and in our theater cases, black suitcases that are a reasonable size as suitcases go, but needless to say are far, far too small for our purposes. Very few cases are not perpetually piled high and overflowing around the edges. This is fine during the season, but when we go on tour and must close the lid, it is quite another story. We throw things out, give them away and then sit on the lid. I've been known to cry on closing night from the anxiety of not being able to close my goddamned case. The hard things cause the problems—ankle and arm weights, foot and back rollers, magic circle (a large metal spring band, pressed between the knees to strengthen inner thigh muscles) and the interminable array of bottles, shampoo, hair spray, baby oil, powder, creams, alcohol and antibiotic creams for our bloody toes.

There are some basic rules for rehearsal clothes. Everything must be soft, old, borrowed, pinned, cut up and oversized. And worn only once—variety is essential. Only new company members wear anything that actually fits, a sure giveaway of their youth. We go through fads: big sweat shirts, Capezio's latest leg warmers, or triple layers of leg warmers. New articles are very suspicious; they contain no personal identity, so the scissors are instantly applied to the neckline (as low as possible, please!). The basic premise is to cover up and keep warm. Layer upon layer is essential so that we can peel off at appropriate intervals when sufficient warmth and confidence for self-exposure is reached. When we are onstage in tutus and leotards, it is the most naked we've been all day. Layers also give a wonderful feeling of possibility; after all, one can always take them off. Adding layers also happens but less frequently; it's a sign that things aren't going so well in the security area.

The one and only time we all strip is for Mr. Balanchine. He demands to see exactly what he is getting. He does not take kindly to paraphernalia. After all, we are hired to show our bodies, so those layers are rather defeating the purpose.

November 28: Well, the Christmas season has begun with our first *Nutcracker* rehearsals. The atmosphere is decidedly different—easier, lighter, less serious and less worried. Six new faces, apprentices, epitomize the new atmosphere—young, eager, watchful and very full-out. I don't doubt that every one of us watching them recalls when we were those very girls. And I think how I now appear as one of those "old girls" who always wore baggy clothes and managed to smile and laugh a lot. How mystical, beautiful, knowing and relaxed they were—and what terrible teachers! And now I am one of them. I could not have a greater sympathy for these new girls, their feelings, and the few years ahead of them. I feel rather like saying to them, "Don't worry; it's hard, but it's great, great fun." I see four years of emotional growing up and learning ahead for them. No four years of a life could be a more interesting growing-up experience than those first years in NYCB.

What do we do in such relaxed rehearsals? Well, I dipped into the pianist's book, *My Contemporaries* by Jean Cocteau, all about Anna de Noailles, Picasso, André Gide, Proust and Raymond Radiguet. I liked poor Modigliani best of all, dying of tuberculosis in poverty at thirty-six after a life of drugs, drink, cafés, friends, Paris and only five to fifteen francs a portrait! I slip momentarily into romantic visions of the Paris of the twenties, overflowing with artists, ideas and poverty—except Proust: "He could afford to be ill." I look up into the rehearsal, the bright lights, beautiful young girls, jewelry, mirrors—we definitely have a very different artistic environment!

So that is what I did in this morning's rehearsal, and I'm paid for it—not bad! I feel a naive nostalgia, if that is possible, for the pure artistic life; poverty. After all, if you're not paid for your art, you need not question your motives.

That reminds me of a dressing-room conversation the other day: If you inherited a million dollars tomorrow, would you stay here and dance? How we all delight in the possibility. The general consensus was, yes, we'd stay, but with a lot more vacations. I'm quite sure that the fact that we are paid slightly diminishes our purity of purpose. We become spoiled and think we are dancing in order to live, rather than living in order to dance. But then we are in America, where money is the sign of success, not in the Paris of the 1920s, when the metaphysics of the soul were discussed. My only complaint is all this work, with no time to sit in cafés and contemplate, drink and smoke. I'm sure we'd be much better with such time as well—but then, as Mr. B. said in an interview in Paris: "We are Americans, and we don't sit and eat; we work all day, every day." I'm sure he did his fair share of Parisian café-sitting in his youth!

For this art form, dancing, thinking should not go beyond steps, toe shoes and ballets. It is best that way. That is how we remember the fifty to sixty ballets in the repertory in a season. People always wonder how we manage to remember so many, but it is not that hard. There are basics.

The first year or so is the hardest; one learns as many as twenty to thirty new ballets, and after that just a few new ones each season. We learn like any student. Our minds are trained to pick up steps and count music. It becomes second nature, just as a college student learns to read quickly and pick out the important points. It's part of our job, that's all.

And so with the condition of the soul. The soul acquires knowledge and is kept going and improved by learning and practice, which are of the nature of movements.

— *Plato,* Theaetetus

I want to go back to the story of Isabelle. I must confess that her liaison with the Duke did not end after that one triumphant meeting. He was not so easily dismissed. He pursued her, and she resisted admirably. But how long could she refuse such determined intent? Besides, she had by now looked in those blue eyes. And so she gave in; they saw each other almost daily for weeks. They talked—they talked and talked. I fear that Isabelle talked the Duke to death. He had never met such a talker. But talking was her defense and her dignity. She maintained them beautifully. But then she began to wonder, and even to worry: this man so famous for seducing young girls had not laid a finger on her.

The subject came up, and he confessed; he was quite happy with their relationship as it was—talking. But then he slyly added that he doubted if it would stay that way. That struck both a spark of excitement and the fear of God in poor Isabelle. Did he have it all planned, all worked out? Did he know the future? Was he really in control?

She began thinking more and more of this "future prospect." She had none of that trembling desire for him that heroines in romantic novels succumb to; how could she desire that which she did not know?

Another thing: not once had he mentioned her body, her looks, her appeal. All talking was kept on a safe, removed level: dancing, dancers, ideas.

Then one night it all began for Isabelle. He became personal, embarrassingly and delightfully personal, with remarks and questions. He knew by now of her inexperience. He delighted in being her first. He had the opportunity to become a god of sorts to her, to introduce her to that of which she knew nothing. He wanted her now, really wanted her; he'd done enough foreplay, more than he'd done for a long time. But he had been wonderfully amused, not bored as before (as he told her later: young girls were best seen and loved, not heard; friends were to be listened to).

By this time, despite all her moral efforts to the contrary, she liked him. He was different, amusing, famous, and he made her feel good, as if she too were famous.

She decided on a condition. She knew that to ask for a ring or marriage was absurd, but she wanted something, some token that she was special. She worked out her speech, her contract. She even went so far as to write it down just to be sure. She felt better after this—more moral, perhaps.

She demanded that he want her, at least for now, totally and uniquely. She knew she could not ask for the results. Maybe she would not want him. But she had to know he did not have a list of other young ballerinas awaiting his conquering. She would not give only to be crossed off the list. He listened, most earnestly and sympathetically, or at least he appeared to—charm goes a long way. He liked it when she confessed to having put her thoughts on paper. To be on paper was a wonderful thing to him, so totally alien a medium for his immortality, one he would never pursue.

He complied with her request; they would embark on a "relationship." They went to dinner to celebrate. As they sat down, he asked Isabelle, "How does it feel—having a relationship?" She laughed, "But it's no different." They returned to his apartment. Her curiosity and nerves far overpowered any amorous feeling. He had stolen some candles from the restaurant; he lit them and played Khachaturian's *Spartacus*—not soft, seductive music, but big, grand, powerful music. She might have known this was a foreshadowing of things to come. The magnificence of the ensuing hours is best left to their two memories; all else would surely profane what was so sacred to Isabelle. But I will say this: as she sat on the big black bed in the corner, with the candles and music, he touched her—he took her hand—and this young girl who had not had a sexual feeling ever for any man was transformed into a trembling mass. The conscious control that she had taught herself for eighteen years was lost totally, completely and magnificently. Only afterwards could she believe that she had been so transformed into pure feeling. She had not known that rational human beings could lose all reason in thirty seconds. Somewhere along the way she meekly offered a suggestion: "Not everything, not everything tonight?" But when he murmured that that was impossible for him, she only too easily acquiesced—and only too easily understood what he meant. And so it began, this wonderful love affair—for she fell in love as only young girls do, with all the intensity and passion that she possessed for everything.

And so Isabelle learned—she was always a quick learner —about love. That pain she had only read about she felt already the next day. Where was he, why didn't he call? He became the source of her existence. He was her existence. All else in her short life was thrown into instant perspective; it was not life at all, only preparation. This was life, this was being alive. This was why one lived. This transformation of mind into feeling was everything; this total loss of reason became her only reason. And she waited each day to lose her reason once again.

There were episodes and whole days of separation and pain, but she adored even her pain. It came from the only worthwhile thing. Everything else had a new value—life, dancing, people. And oh, how she danced, how she jumped. She developed a new spin, a new energy came. Only she knew its source, and she coveted and guarded her secret like a jewel. And there were good times. They laughed, they chewed bones—how he loved to watch her chew bones, her delicate little face lost in a mass of red meat and burnt edges. There was the time the landlord and the neighbors came rapping at the door to save whoever was being killed—their togetherness was most vocal. How they laughed after that.

Afterwards Isabelle often wondered if the moments themselves were greater or the memory of them. At least the memory did not pass, while the moments passed all too fast. Life whizzed by; she no longer had time to recollect it. Her notebooks to this day retain the story of her desperate attempt to hold together her self, her mind, her reason, her order, her morals.

Give me Brahms, give me Beethoven, give me Bach—what a joy to dance to such music—what a joy!

—Larry Stevens

November 30: It is Sunday night, a special night to us because tomorrow is our free day—the one day of the week when we try to make up for all lost living time: laundry, bills, friends, meals, sleep. We just closed with a magnificent *Stars and Stripes.* Since it is the last ballet of the week we are all tired, very tired, yet we muster up more energy than ever from the inspiration that afterwards we will be free. Heather Watts and Peter Martins pulled out all the stops tonight. The wings were filled with cheering, smiling faces, applauding and yelling with delight. I hope the audience was as thrilled as we were. Peter's eyes constantly glanced into the wings as if for more food. It worked somehow; we loved them, and they rose to the occasion. There was a wonderful, warm family feeling—it happens more often than you might imagine. No more complaints or axes or anxieties, but all pure goodwill flowing out for the success of *Stars and Stripes,* of the evening, and of NYCB. We were magnificent tonight.

Somehow this reminded me of a rather special closing night in New York a year ago last spring. An old faithful fan was there as usual. He had a gift for a few of us; he called it a doll he had made, but it looked to me rather more like a scourer for the dishes. It now hangs on my wall, with a little scrawled note:

Made with loving, caring hands for lovely Toni Bentley, lovely Elfin Fairy Ballerina. Thank you, Toni dear, for so very many beautifully artistic performances, which have given me so very much delight and joy. I'm so very beholden to you for all the long, hard, painful years of sustained effort and work in perfecting your beautiful art and talents. With admiration and

loving respect

Guy T. Moore, consulting engineer

And thank you so much, Mr. Moore—your gift and note have gotten me through three subsequent seasons. They prove that sometimes one of us corps people is noticed, and it makes it all more than worthwhile—thank you, Mr. Moore.

December 1: A day beginning with too little sleep. Today I'm frustrated over nothing. I search for an object and find numerous ones (one always can, can't one?), yet I know they have no value. I am empty, purely and simply empty, although in fact I'm extra glamorous today: exotic makeup and a turban on my head in an attempt to fill the void. Glamour not only does not fill the void but makes it worse. Each time I look in a mirror I see a pathetic attempt to find beauty in her who feels none. This is my search for today —for beauty. And God knows it's all over the place—in Vivaldi, in dancing, in faces, in Théophile Gautier, whom I read. Yet it only makes me emptier. It is sad that what fills my whole life at times means so little today. I know artists turn their sadness to art, but I cannot dance here on the page.

Perhaps this is the anticlimax after the joyous time I had dancing last week and that Sunday-night *Stars and Stripes.* I was all smiles and laughs and energy. Now for three nights we don't dance, so that nonsensical flow of good humor must be stifled. I want to laugh and cannot. If I danced, I could laugh. To live and to laugh require a reason. But dancing is so close to one's guts that it has no reason and yet it needs none; it's physical, and as a source of good cheer it is endless.

I saw *Raging Bull* yesterday and of course thought of the tragic sadness and frailty of those whose life is based on the physical—fighters and dancers. Damn this body of ours, it goes eventually, and even if one moves on in life and survives, that physical career will always have been one's high point. How could it be otherwise in retirement—early retirement for us, at thirty or forty. One is so aware it is due to inability, physical inability. What greater reminder of one's slow decay toward death? That coming to terms with mind and body ability is an inevitable, frightening prospect for all of us.

We have the constant reminder of such a day before us with the example of older dancers and the varied choices they make. Some decide one day this is their last perform-ance and leave with a certain amount of sad glory; others continue on, doing less and less as their capacity wanes, often in a great deal of physical pain and God knows what amount of emotional pain. It's like growing old far too early; instead of one's mind dwindling, one's body dwin-dles, with one's mind totally intact, filled with the same desire and energy as ever—probably more.

Unlike some European and Soviet companies, we are not provided for in retirement. We get no pension, no security and no retirement plan. After all, at thirty-five or forty we are still able-bodied in the eyes of society. The fact that one has given one's entire being—energy, time, body, thought, care and love—from age eight to age forty to one's art makes no difference. Doesn't a dancer at forty deserve some respect and reward, or at least some future security? A dancer has given all he has got; he has squeezed himself dry of all creative juices every day of his life, and finally his body says, no more. He cannot continue. What other pro-fessional becomes so literally unable to continue his career?

Yet college professors and government workers get pensions, and dancers do not.

Our work is taken from us through no fault of our own, except maybe the fault of choosing to dance at all. But nobody warns a ten-year-old that he will be finished at forty, and what ten-year-old would listen? I doubt that even one of us would not choose to do it again, for we are believers. No dancer will deny the value, the total value, of his dedication. Who could ever say after giving so much of himself—more than he ever conceived existed—that it was not the highest possible pursuit, to use and shape all one's energy to create beauty?

On the other hand, our mothers all have serious doubts. Someone said to me recently that he thought boys and girls danced as a form of revenge on their mothers. The most successful of us have traumatic times, and who could suffer more than our mothers, who can see only the bloody toes, the injustice, the fatigue, the tears and the loneliness. Perhaps a certain tendency to masochism or at least the acceptance of both physical and emotional pain is a prerequisite for dancing, for the absolute belief and dedication that is dancing. Mothers, whose choice was to have a family, understandably have a difficult time conceiving of the totally different forms of reward that we receive—being on stage, moving to music, the magic of lights and applause. If they have not known it themselves, how can they understand that it is all worthwhile?

My mother worries incessantly that I'm doing the wrong

thing. Only those stage-door mothers who themselves dreamed of dancing professionally could forever continue to encourage their teary-eyed, injured, overworked little girls. Recently the mother of a young girl who was auditioning for the school took one look at the bleeding feet and gossiping children and ran out of the building with her daughter in tow. When I have a daughter, I too will keep her clear of competitive ballet schools.

I've got a confession I've made to no one. I was a neurotic eater. I can admit it now only because I'm normal again. I eat every day. Yes indeed, I tackle a full array of foods, although at home, in my studio, my refrigerator is empty except for diet soda, juice, skim milk, seltzer water and cat food. It keeps life simple to have no choice.

I went through years of neurotic eating when often each day began with the challenge to fast, to eat nothing. I'm thin. I've always been thin, and the members of my family are thin, but at ballet school, before I ever gained an ounce of excess weight, I became fearful of doing so. I saw it all around me. How could I know and trust myself enough to know that would not happen to me? At some point everyone seemed to gain weight. I attributed it to indulgence; the thought of oncoming womanhood never occurred to me, and even if it did, womanhood as such had no right to infringe on my dancer's body! I suppose every dancer in competitive circumstances these days has had her bout of neurotic eating habits: fasting, binges, etc. A few become anorexic. I never did. Something in me prevented it, yet I feel quite experienced in that disease. It's indicative of the desire to control everything: one's body, one's mind, one's future, one's impulses. It is a unique experience in the art of self-discipline, and except for its detrimental effects, a great teacher. It involves solitude, thought, planning and giving in to no one's pleas, especially one's own.

When I see very thin, anorexic-type girls, my heart goes out to them. God knows no one understands them. But to all those who deal with them, I say let them alone. No one outside of her own mind can change or affect the decision such a girl has reached within herself. She must live it out, find out, learn for herself—and with luck she'll not suffer too much damage. After all, it is a self-inflicted disease. I think the rapidly thinning girl at the worst of times is more productive and happy and sane than those who take the opposite road to adolescent problems—overeating and indulgence. I've known both, and from my experience the girl who has too much self-control is on a greater road to discovery than the girl who is losing her thoughts in cream cakes. The anorexic has absorbed a great knowledge. She has control—some control—over her destiny and has taken responsibility for that destiny.

December 3: The first snowflakes fell in the theater this afternoon, heralding the *Nutcracker* season, and retaining a pensive ill humor around here is impossible. Suddenly every doorway, every elevator and every hallway is full of squirming little bodies. Not only are there two whole casts of children, A and B (no discrimination intended), but each child has two parents. I'm deliberating which are more amusing—the kids or the parents. Too few of the children are innocent. Little Marie seems to be, arriving late to rehearsal in tiny yellow sweat pants, golden curls and a well-loaded little belly. But for the most part, they are all horribly adult-like and self-conscious, with flowers in their hair, rouge on their cheeks, and all the rehearsal paraphernalia in miniature. The little boys are quite dangerous, never walking down narrow corridors but always running at top speed, tripping us older, slower folk.

The familiar sign is up in one elevator: "No *Nutcracker* children or parents in this elevator." It goes predictably unheeded. I overheard some remarks: "Well, Mom, Mr. B. didn't pay as much attention to me as before." "Well, dear, it's your second year; he thinks you know already." Like hell he does. He's just given up.

There is the usual charming confrontation between the little Prince and Mr. B. discussing the Prince's pantomime. Mr. B. always asks others to translate for him when the child doesn't respond: "I speak Russian. We say 'I there.' You say 'There I.'" And Mr. B. proceeds with the perfect pantomime of the Prince's story. Year after year it is always the same.

Walking alone down a hallway, I feel two huge caressing hands around my neck. Peter Martins is behind me. I'm not sure if it is a blessing or a curse to live with such prospects each day. I suppose in any working situation the men and women flirt—but truly, we have the cream of the crop!

We have other opportunities, too—men conscious of dancers love to stop them in the street and arrange dates. But is this any way to meet a mate? Of course we are obvious with our turned-out toes and pulled-back ponytails. Naturally we can meet other people, but we have to make an extra effort, both to find the time and to make the conversation. Many, especially the younger girls, do not have enough desire or energy to do it. Those who wish to meet people do. We have a number of parties, especially on tour, and I've made some wonderful friends that way. But too often meeting an "outside" person involves the usual cross-examination: Where are you from? How long have you been dancing? What's it like working with Balanchine? What did you dance tonight? We have a lot of jokes about pre-recording our answers. Of course people are curious (they'd better be!). We are unique, yet on a human-to-human level, this is very dull and finite in possibility.

Personally, I prefer people who know nothing about ballet so we can skip the awe and adulation and move on to good times. We are not objects of chiffon and lace. Time spent with some fanatic balletomane is dull indeed to most of us. We have dreams about a wonderful guy who hates ballet and has never heard of Balanchine.

I gather someone was around today asking some of the girls for information about our lives, but she was not given any solid answers. An interview, after all, is simply another chance to perform and increase our enigmatic aspect. Why should we tell some stranger about the lives we live? We are proud, very proud, of our position and intend to retain our privacy.

It's just a half-hour since I washed the first season's snow-flakes from my cleavage—yes, some of us almost have one, and yes, the snowflakes fall straight down it. In fact those goddamn snowflakes get everywhere—all over the theater, in our bags, in our hair, even at home. Often odd flakes turn up months later. Well, we are in for five solid weeks of it —forty sold-out performances of *The Nutcracker*.

It is the annual reminder of one's age and the passing of the years. For us who know the ballet inside out, the talk is of the years. This is my ninth *Nutcracker* season, including my four years as a hoop when I was in the school. The signs are everywhere. I see last year's little Marie as a boy poli-chinelle and the mice moving on but not out of the lime-light. As we all do, I suppose—from school star to corps de ballet. The boy on his knees under the bed, moving it around the stage, danced the Prince in the school's work-shop performance last May. Now he is bed boy. Last year's tiny girls have grown tall and bosomy and flirtatious.

But *Nutcracker* is still wonderful. I still get chills when the tree grows tall and the little bed floats around the stage, especially when the trap door is open and threatens disaster. No one speaks of the beauty; that is for silent appreciation. *Nutcracker* becomes the object of laughter, and how the jokes flow!

For the first time ever there is a boy hoop—one little Chinese boy—and Madame Pourmel, our fussy Russian wardrobe mistress, would not let him wear a girl's costume, so he has a new one of his own! We company girls, on the other hand, must fit the same costumes year after year or we are subjected to acute embarrassment. Our growth must be internal, not external.

We all have a love-hate relationship with little Madame Pourmel; she is so incredibly fussy, organized and meticulous, yelling if our hands are on our costumes, or we arrive late for a fitting. But we know it's her job, and it is her love that keeps our costumes as beautiful as they are. She has trouble understanding our youthful lack of respect for her instruments—our tutus. We do not appreciate the work, time, detail and historic value of what we wear. But then our job is to dance, and hers is to clothe us. But we forgive her her rampages. We have to; she's been there from the beginning, and no doubt will outlast us all. Like all the Russians we live with—Balanchine, Danilova, and others—her endless devotion and energy are truly timeless; we Americans have no such historic persistence.

Each time we are fitted for a new costume, it is pinned, hitched and sewn precisely to fit us. In the wardrobe all day every day there is endless fixing, stretching, cleaning and altering. Such care is surely one of the few remaining arts left over from the old world in our modern machine-run age. Everything is done by hand!

December 4: The first *Nutcracker* is greeted in the dressing room with a large bottle of Chablis. We drain it.

A bra discussion is underway. This is a very unusual and difficult article for us all. We so rarely use it. Only a select few have any daily need. The rest of us wear one only for white-leotard ballets. Bras are a problem. None is small enough, stretchy enough or comfortable enough. We usually resort to Teenform training bras, the ones most girls wear in the sixth grade. Today a new Teenform was discovered. We all examine it for color, transparency, price. Tomorrow each of us will buy three or four. Such a find may not come again soon.

I have a totally free day tomorrow—a fluke. It is Cast B's turn. Such a prospect instills a great joie de vivre in us all. We can stay out a little later, eat and drink a little more, sleep a little later, go to the movies—in short, we are free to live a little more. What a treat!

I just read in the paper: "Money is adulthood, but above all, money is choice." Maybe that is why dancers are and will be eternally underpaid. We have no choice; we choose to have no choice. In fact, it would be impossible to dance if we had a choice.

A lover once said to me, "If I could have even half the power over you that this Balanchine has . . ."

Most women have two important men in their lives— their father and their lover. We have three. Mr. Balanchine is our leader, our president, our mother, our father, our friend, our guide, our mentor, our destiny.

He knows all, sees all, and controls all—all of us—most often by saying very, very little. He seems to believe in self-discovery, and at times that is hell—when one knows that he knows but will not tell. Trusting him forces us to trust ourselves. He is our third parent, the parent of our adulthood, when so many people have none at all. We are all his children, but his adult children—his working, dancing, performing children. His power over us is unique. I doubt any girl has passed through the world of NYCB without feeling the deep influence of Mr. B. upon her and upon the course of her life. He has our admiration. He loves us all. He adores our beauty and extends it out of all conceivable proportion in his ballets. What more could a girl ask of a man than such an appreciation?

He walks into a room: all layers of warmers are removed, silence is instant, and the sweat flows faster, the legs go higher and the front of the studio is filled with aspiring ballerinas. He sees all, so it is said, instantly. As an apprentice one hears that he needs to see only one demi-plié, and he knows how you dance, how you live, who you are and what your future is. Each night word is passed around to tell us whether he is present or not. Usually he is, but a predictable relief and freedom of spirit abound when he is not. The air is lifted instantly when he is not present, yet no one prefers it.

He is wonderfully human. I still have trouble remembering that. He talks about the weather, eats, drinks, and no doubt does other normal things. I once talked to him about champagne. Immediately I was relaxed: we had common ground! Trying to come to terms with his enigma only enhances it in the end. He becomes more, not less. He doesn't seem to lack anything human, spiritual, emotional or practical.

When he speaks, all ears are pricked, and we close in on him. His every word is sucked into each of us as prophetic, though afterwards we often cannot find the meaning—perhaps because it is so simple.

His life is our example. With dancing, he is direct and simple. He wants to see the steps, the movement, each movement, with all the energy that exists—*now, now, now!* "What are you waiting for? What are you saving for? Now is all there is." "You must practice being happy, as you must practice everything, and you will be." Faster, faster, everything faster. His voice echoes its daily repetitions: "If you rehearse sloppy, you will dance sloppy. You rehearse how you will do it."

The plié deeper, the jump higher, the arms bigger. Everything bigger—never, ever can we do enough. "No, no, no, dear, move, dear." Classes with him are a lesson in exaggeration—jumps landing in grand plié, legs held up forever. In short, energy is the key, the source, the message. Rehearse your energy. Tendus so fast there is a blur between the opening and closing of the leg. No breath—there is no time

—then laughter and grins as we all feel the impossibility of his demands and the refusal of our legs to do more.

No place for vanity here. "Just do it, dear, just do it. Don't worry, just do." And from this preaching and teaching comes our beauty, not a placid classic beauty—"Gisellititis," he calls it—but big, broad, exaggerated stretches, extreme pure beauty—energetic beauty.

There is, in the end, the final product—no cheating, no cover-ups. One is bare, naked, exposed. Once on stage it is done. One's work, care, energy and output are in the raw, exposed to three thousand pairs of eyes and one pair that sees more than all the others put together. What you eat shows, how you slept shows, your love and care show, your destiny shows, and we know it. And how we love it, that exposure.

A dancer, a man, once said to me that he can tell how a person makes love by the way he or she dances. After all, dancing is rather like lovemaking. We give to receive and receive to give. That is why we need applause; it is our only feedback!

European audiences are the most consistent in their tributes, perhaps only out of politeness and good manners, but it pays off. I doubt anyone will ever forget closing night in Copenhagen two years ago. A standing ovation, showers of flowers in little carefully wrapped bouquets. They screamed and yelled and were divine. We had such fun. And when an audience finally coaxes Mr. B. out—with our help; it takes both—the moment is magnificent. We, his dancers, become his onstage audience, applauding and smiling, and very few eyes are dry. When he bows in front of the curtain, the backstage furor is equal to that on the other side of the orchestra pit.

The moment, special moments, are what make it all worthwhile—Suzanne's daredevil balance, Peter Martins when he is on (or even when he's off!), a debut, an outrageous mistake in *Swan Lake,* even a slip or fall can be monumental and magnificent. Stories abound of idiosyncratic performances when someone overslept or got her period on stage (it has happened more often than you might think).

December 5: We have a rehearsal with Peter Martins today for one of his new ballets. He begins by pulling his bulky sweater over his head. His blond hair is ruffled. He is like Apollo just awakened.

"That's good . . . Well, someone has got to think so." He grins.

We all laugh. Is he really funny? Or could he say anything and charm us?

There is lots and lots of discussion. Peter is admired but not feared, so we and he all offer suggestions and criticisms: "Oh, that's like Jerry." "That's like my last ballet." "That's like *Serenade*; let's do it!" We are working under the silent presence of Mr. B. as always. Instead of the stigma of imitation, there is a feeling of unquestionable righteousness when Balanchine steps are used.

Peter is thrilled like a little boy when the sequences are connected and flow smoothly. Does he know how good he looks, smiling and wide-eyed? There is a flirtatiousness in the air as he takes each of us by the hand and guides us to our place in line.

Peter rarely raises his voice and has a constant flow of ideas. We accomplish a lot in only one hour. He criticizes himself very little. He is not serious about himself. He gets away with everything and anything.

He has special choreographing outfits: very tight blue jeans and T-shirts bearing some message or other; he doesn't need one with his name on the back as many of us have. He has an all-white outfit: white jeans, white sweater, white sneakers. He looks like Mr. Clean. He wears a watch on one wrist, a turquoise band on the other, both setting off his huge encompassing hands. He often looks at himself in the mirror and straightens a stray curl. He has no shame, no self-consciousness; he just wants to keep the image perfect.

He asks our opinion: "Is it too hard, too fast, too repetitive, too many bourrées?" He receives twenty answers simultaneously. His rehearsals are the most relaxed of all our choreographers', perhaps because we can appeal to his vanity, and he to ours. This keeps everyone bubbling with humor and hopes. We cannot regard him purely as "the choreographer."

December 7: I'm "free" for three days, two without class. I no longer feel like a dancer. My body is lost, so I took class today. As always, one day without dancing and one feels one is no longer a dancer. After all, there is no proof that one can dance unless one is dancing! I leave the theater; downstairs by the guard the couch is piled high with bouquets and boxes of flowers addressed to unknown names. The ten-year-olds receive flowers daily. We get none. Oh to be a young star!

> *Smoothest ice,*
> *A paradise,*
> *to him who is a dancer nice.*
>
> —*Nietzsche,* Joyful Wisdom

I was talking last night to one of the extra-talented, extra-beautiful dancers in the company. She was rather melancholy: "I don't know what I'll do after dancing. I've no hobbies, no other talents, not enough curiosity." All I could say was, "But you're so beautiful." To me and the world that is far, far more than enough. But to her?

Tomorrow we are having "the most important meeting in the history of NYCB." Management has rejected all our proposals and has offered their own. "There may be a strike vote." Mr. B. has been told and was predictably upset, emotional, saying what he is always saying: "I do my best, I try; you can go elsewhere if you don't like it; if you want to run the company I'll leave and take my ballets." Oh God, how awful we feel; we only want enough money to pay the rent. Many of the younger kids simply cannot afford it. Their parents have to help them. Mr. B. takes it personally, of course. We are his company, his creation, his tools; without him we are nothing, and without us—well, he needs us, but he can always find dancers. The question seems rather basic: do we want to fight for our own pockets, or do we give a little for him? We will see tomorrow, but God knows that he is greater than we, and we love him. We will show him that—and maybe scrimp a little more.

December 8: I have just come from the union meeting. About seventy people out of a hundred showed up at the Renaissance Room of the Holiday Inn. We sat in rows of chairs with the long banquet table raised before us. Only coffee and water graced the white cloth on the empty table. We began placidly, listening to explanations of the proposals at hand. All went smoothly until the real question was raised: to strike or not to strike. Was this the time to act? NYCB is in the black and as "rich" as it will ever be, but should we push our money demands at the risk—a sure risk —of hurting Mr. B.? Should we in effect put not only ourselves but him out of work? Is this the time to do that to him, when he has just had two major operations and is planning a Tchaikovsky festival? The room vibrated with tension, emotional outbursts, speeches and tears. There was little, very little, comic relief at this meeting. Peter Martins made a speech against the strike and was shouted down, though his charm, calm and manner retained their ever-present appeal. With the talk of his someday taking over NYCB, I saw a step in history—his being there with us, as a dancer, listening, speaking and thinking of our rights. The discussion split into two sides, the emotional cries for Balanchine at all costs, and those who persisted in disregarding the possible effects and sticking with our financial demands and need for money and power. The principal dancers were all there, thank God.

Our final decision was to reject the management's current proposal and postpone any strike-vote action until Mr. B. has been informed of everything and we know his view. The vote was unanimous and instant on the last. Like children, his children, we feel sure and safe in trusting him. No matter what he feels, first we must know, and then we will think again. To act without his knowledge of all we ask for would have left every soul in the room anxious and lost.

There was endless discussion of Mr. B.'s position. Someone said that he is neither us nor union nor management, but a world unto himself and therefore excludable. Another instantly replied that he is not a world unto himself but is the ruler and creator of the world we inhabit. His word will be final.

I know I continue to harp on the emotional aspect and primary place Mr. B. has over what is pure economic bartering. But as I've said, and I'll repeat it again and again: NYCB is unique in the world; it is the creation of fifty years of one man's ideas. What other "company" must consider such an aspect? The Metropolitan Opera strikes, actors

strike, American Ballet Theatre strikes, firemen strike—
why not fight for yourself 100 percent of the way? For all
of them, they are rightfully supreme in importance. But we
have a second party to ourselves who is supreme. Balanchine
created NYCB from nothing.

So much for our meeting. We emerge in unison after
three hours and disperse in our different solitary directions
to fill the remainder of our free day.

*In the mental discipline I had recently begun, and of which I
already felt the good effects, stability equipoise and tranquillity
were the prerequisites. I said to myself, "Tranquillity, tranquillity." As on the racquet ball court I said, "Dance, dance, dance!"*

—*Saul Bellow,* Humboldt's Gift

I want to go back to little Isabelle. The full tide of first love
did not last. It could not last by the very laws it stood upon.
Such passion contains and demands its own demise. Isabelle
was learning to live. Before the Duke, she was happy, as
happy as she'd ever been, dancing, working and bouncing
about. Her days were as full as they had ever been; so were
her thoughts. Then the Duke broke into that world—a
happy functional world, although it was only one level of
many. He raised her existence to a new plane. He introduced
love into her life. Then he moved on—not on to other girls
(although no doubt that, too) but on in the world, around
the world. Such men are unsettled and never remain anywhere for long. Isabelle was spared the base humiliation of

another woman; nevertheless, she faced separation. But her energy was so strong, it could handle that, and she would love and believe in him till death. Never since has she felt such total belief in one man, and never since has she encountered one so unworthy. He was unobtainable and unpossessable. He no longer belonged to Isabelle, she knew, but he belonged to no one else either. The number of girls he knew made no difference. He was invulnerable to the persuasion of love, but vulnerable to love by being unpossessed. So she wrote to him, sent him cookies in fine, wrapped boxes, and retained her faith for two years.

But unintentionally, for she wanted her love to remain as it was, she grew up. She had to. She never lost her faith, but life constantly confronted her with new discoveries. Slowly the faith she had in the Duke slipped, and real life became unavoidable. She never lost the intensity she had felt, but the forms changed. Questioning became her daily existence. Life and death, goals and accomplishments, self-cultivation and philosophy became her sources. She found herself alone with her love, but suddenly the rest of the world joined her. The Duke did not join her, but Wagner did.

Opera had held no meaning for her before. Then one night she stood at the back of the Metropolitan Opera for *La Bohème,* then for *Lohengrin, Götterdämmerung, Tosca, La Traviata.* She became obsessed, standing every night (and every morning before class for tickets). Wagner, and he alone, understood her intensity of love. She found a companion, but he did not touch her body, only her senses. So instead of joy and smiles and vivacious laughter, she became solitary, quiet, tranquil and constantly fearful.

People worried. Her parents despaired. They viewed this transition from "living" to Wagner as one obsession filling the gap of another. But she knew her love was in abeyance and waiting. The aim was to retain the feeling, the plateau, the intensity that had been born. What mattered was not ever to lose what she had been given. It's a pity that the Duke did not know, could not know what he had instilled in Isabelle. Later he learned of all her doings but was strangely unaffected by what he had created.

Isabelle met the Duke years after, when she was fully restored to life as it was, but his effect on her was the same; it always will be, she knows that. She only wonders why. He is her unreasonableness. He was the source of it and remains the sole instigator of it still. She has known other loves more lasting, more tender, more giving, more sensitive, but in this her love for the Duke stands alone. He represents her only loss of reason. She can see no reason on earth to love him as she did, and that alone is the greatest reason of all to her. For some other lovers she could write lists of good points, good traits, strong, lasting, productive qualities. For him her page is empty, but she cries when she is with him in total joy. The more strongly she feels him next to her, the more she knows he will be gone —poof—like a dream. And like the little romantic that she is, she would rather have that closeness for one minute and an eternity of solitude than never to have known such feeling.

And how does dancing come into this story? It held her back. Otherwise she would have chased her beloved around the world. But she had the only good reason on earth not to do so. His evasiveness was surely a reason, but she believed she would conquer it. To leave dancing, however, would have been to leave herself—all she was, all she had done in her short life, all she cared about. So the affair ended, and she danced. She knew that if she left dancing for him she would arrive at his doorstep, at his feet, helpless, lost and incomplete. She would never lower her love to such a level. He deserved a ballerina, a goddess, not a grasping girl. I think they call this a sense of self. Well, Isabelle had it—still has it. Something taught her that— something about losing all to find all.

December 9: The atmosphere at the theater was thick today. Between John Lennon's death, Balanchine and the contract, we've become a tearful, thoughtful group. Rehearsals take place in a daze of thoughts, emotions and group discussions. The dressing rooms are full of smoke, coffee cups, newspapers, and endless mimeographs of contract information. We are at a high point of literacy. Notebooks are seen under many arms, petitions are signed, and endless tête-à-têtes take place. Though the issues are sad and precarious, the unity they have inspired is truly heartwarming. I've never felt such a part of a family working for common goals.

Hear ye, hear ye, NYCB has its first taste of democracy and is enjoying it immensely. Our lives in the theater are so totally guided and ordained every day that now, with our only chance for self-expression, our fight for a better contract, all of our minds and bodies unite and function as never before. People are talking, really talking, not gossiping, competing or sewing ribbons. Nothing like a common cause. We are alone in so many ways when we dance, but here we are a family and friends. We go on stage knowing that the girl in the wings feels as we do at least on something —and that is rare around here!

At yesterday's meeting, kids were standing up and making speeches before they had the chance to realize what they were doing. Every speech ended with a sudden self-conscious apology: "I didn't intend to make a speech." "I didn't think I was involved." Such a meeting is the only time when we are together as a group—as people, not as dancers, or rather as dancers who are people first. Most of us didn't even know we were people as well.

And so yesterday ten or twenty people exposed themselves, their opinions, their values, their thoughts to us— and the sympathy and willingness to listen and respond was unbelievable. Other precedents were broken, too. The hierarchy, the only hierarchy we know, of principal dancers, soloists and corps was totally broken down. Principals were shouted down by new corps members and yielded admirably! We were true equals when it came to discussing our rights. And so democracy takes hold and is grasped like a new toy within our little world—our dictatorship, our benevolent dictatorship.

But Balanchine triumphed, as he should, as he always will. It is the only way we will have it. We were totally and beautifully unanimously in his favor. NYCB is the only solid cause and creation I know. Would every person on earth had such a monument to believe in!

December 10: My cat was sick last night, and I spent this morning at the animal hospital. Pets are dancers' children, our brothers and sisters and lovers. We come home to them, and they do not tell us to keep in line or lose weight. They love us fat or thin. We can feed them instead of ourselves. Mr. B. is known as a cat man. He tells us to dance like a pussycat, jump like a pussycat—smooth, lithe, intelligent, soft, graceful and purring all the while. Suzanne has at least nine cats, but most of us have only one or two. There are some dogs, but with all the walking time required, they are not very practical. Cats are as we should be—independent, giving, beautiful, interesting to observe. They go with us everywhere possible—to Saratoga and Washington. The bus trips are family affairs with no exceptions—cats, dogs, even birds. We share stories and information about care. Dancing, contracts and pets are our common ties.

One of our more attractive company members has just confessed an affection for me. Funny, I was so full of joie de vivre before knowing of his affection, and now I am sad, knowing that it will go unrequited.

I just finished watching *The Nutcracker* from out front. It was overwhelming and beautiful. The perspectives are so strange from the two sides of the curtain. The stage looks small and very conquerable from the wings, but from the first ring it looks huge, untouchable and impossible. And the lights, which are merely bright when seen from the theater's darkness, are blinding from the wings.

I had the usual reaction we all have when we venture onto the other side of the curtain, that everyone, every snowflake, every flower, is so individual and easily seen, and every slip is so obvious. Yet the predictable corps feeling of safety in numbers does indeed exist, so while everyone tries desperately to stand out and shine, we also feel a certain protection amongst the masses. Out front, I notice every strangely cocked head, floppy foot and odd facial expression. Oh God, I wonder how I must look out there. The one thing I'll never see is me! No doubt that's just as well. We have a general horror of photographs. Indeed, I think we have a very limited conception of how we appear. Occasional films, TV shows or videotapes always produce covered eyes, laughter, defensive comments and much silent contemplation. There are a few dancers who have their performances videotaped to watch for improvement—what masochism! Just like those who remain after performances to rehearse and repair the evening's mistakes. The general opinion is that we can work all day but once on stage, that's it; it's too late. So for God's sake, enjoy it then—it's the only time we go unjudged by that horrendous mirror!

"Wait a bit," she cried, "so you can't dance? Not at all? Not even one step? And yet you talk of the trouble you've taken to live? You told a fib there, my boy, and you shouldn't do that at your age. How can you say that you've taken any trouble to live when you won't even dance?"

—*Hermann Hesse,* Steppenwolf

Any moments spent by dancers in movement are glorious, and one is free and totally oneself (with perhaps one eye on keeping in line, though at NYCB we don't worry about lines too much). But what is bad is standing, waiting interminably in rows as border decoration to the centerpiece. The fourth movement of *Symphony in C* is famous for the wait through the entrance of the dancers who were in the first, second and third movements. This is the first part a new company member receives, this fourth movement, and it's frightful— shot out of a cannon at full speed for two minutes, then waiting on one leg for what feels like twenty. What an introduction to corps life and the art of humility! That poor little leg and foot go through numerous metamorphoses of feeling, from excruciating pain to total numbness.

The thought processes while this is going on are entirely different from those when one is dancing. When one is in motion, one listens and reacts; no thought is needed. When one is standing, everything from the step we do twenty minutes from now to tomorrow's schedule to the pile of laundry waiting in the sink upstairs races through one's mind. I often think of plugging those fourth movement girls into brain readers; the comparison of their unearthly angelic appearance and their thoughts would be ludicrous!

Thinking is not a becoming stage image; the concentration and introspection that accompany the reasoning process are most un-ballerina-like. Perhaps our ethereal appearance is achieved not because of our high level of consciousness but because of having none at all! Our training to separate body and mind is much in evidence in the baby-ballerina types whose muscles respond with a maturity and discipline far ahead of their years. We have a name for this: we say it's "in the muscle." Hence the muscles are the rulers and respond immediately to a command. Turning is a good example of this phenomenon. Some people are "natural turners" who can turn every day—always have, always will —whereas others of us are emotional turners. We know every secret, every placement, every ingredient for that perfect turn, but if we are distracted in any way, we fall. If someone applauds me, I'm finished. I turn best straight out of bed. In that early-morning lack of consciousness I just whip turns off, but by eight o'clock when I'm on display I just pray that no one applauds, at least until I'm finished!

December 12: Three old stagehands rush to the wings from their poker game to watch the little dolls in the first act of

Nutcracker. At the beginning of the second act, a young bearded stagehand stands alone in the fourth wing with the Sugar Plum Fairy. He is her only company before she floats on stage. He is in baggy old pants and a T-shirt that reads: "We do it on cue."

In the backstage office there is a copy of *Eugene Onegin,* a TV set, a refrigerator full of beer, and a scruffy old quote: "We the willing, led by the unknowing, are doing the impossible for the ungrateful. We have done so much with so little for so long, we are now qualified to do anything with nothing!"

The stagehands are the only "real" people backstage with us, and what a mixture they are—old and young, slim and rotund, married and single, bearded and clean-shaven. They drink, joke, laugh, watch the ball game or *Kojak,* and rush to the wings to pull at scenery, fix a blown-out light or catch a debut.

We dancers are fairly oblivious to them. They are the scenery, necessary and always there. A few of us talk and joke with them, but still we complain of no real men around. Yet they are very real men and most sensitive and perceptive if they are "allowed" our friendship. They wink, hand out candy, comment on our new eyelashes, get us rosin for our shoes and catch us in the wings from a flying exit.

I've talked to many of them, and they all say the same two things—that we are all quite intimidating and quite beautiful, and that we live in a world of our own. They have never worked with such a strange group of dancers, all so young and dreamy and dedicated. Modern dancers are far more gregarious. The stagehands find us rather frightening and incomprehensible. The only contact they have with many of us is in the form of complaints: the lights are too hot, there is too much snow, the stage is too slippery. We are true princesses. I suppose we are brought up this way; we are, after all, Balanchine princesses: "Women are everything," he says.

The stagehands provide our setting. They drop the snow, raise the tree, put the swans on the lake and the spotlight on us. We have never been without such tender graces, so we take them for granted; we expect them as if coming from heaven.

I once hung around after closing night on tour and watched twenty-five stagehands work and sweat until 4:00 A.M., rolling and packing scenery, costumes and lights. And then, exhausted and happy to be finished, they began partying—smoking, drinking and laughing. Stagehands are great sports fans and obsessed by little machines, everything from wrenches and screwdrivers to the latest minicomputers, electric clocks and lighters. I guess every profession has its tools. We have leotards, toe shoes and makeup.

It is different with the musicians in our orchestra. I am not alone in knowing by sight only perhaps two or three of them. We simply do not mix. They travel between their lounge downstairs and the orchestra pit and are never seen at stage level. They travel unseen. The conductor's hands as he leads them are our only proof that they exist. Our conductors, Mr. Irving and Mr. Fiorato, on the other hand, are more a part of the ballet than of the orchestra. They are often present at rehearsals, travel with us on tour and "live" backstage with us.

December 14: I got tickets for some starry-eyed out-of-towners last night and indulged in a late-night outing with them after the performance. I was disappointed—very disappointed. They looked hesitantly but eagerly at me, sat up very straight and asked, "What's the gossip?" I don't believe half of the gossip I hear, would never pass it on, and consider any that is true far too personal to tell outsiders. Besides, it is so unimportant. The facts, the vision, the true daily realities of our life are far, far more interesting.

Then they asked if someone puts on our makeup. No, we do our own, and no one teaches us how. The art of self-beautification with makeup is in the air. The theater exudes such talents. We practice, experiment and learn from one another, and there is not one among us, male or female, who is untalented in the art. While we put on our makeup, we have Coke and coffee, cigarettes, and rock and roll on the radio at three hundred decibels. We stand, we sit, we prance, we pose, we turn, we twirl, we admire and we condemn. It's part of the show—a part totally our own to do as we wish. Great fun indeed, night after night. We become most proficient with practice—from a scrubbed naked face to full lavish makeup and hair in half an hour. And when performance is over, one handful of baby oil and the vision is removed in five seconds. We are proud of it; it's our job and our pleasure. We use the same eyelashes (top only) over and over; in fact, getting used to new eyelashes is a dreadful ordeal!

December 16: They have chosen the children for *A Midsummer Night's Dream.* Inevitably, because there are so many fewer parts, many who dance in *The Nutcracker* were not chosen. The cast sheets went up, and tears flowed. A little girl was overheard to ask, "Can a twelve-year-old have a nervous breakdown?" They learn early, these little dancers. They grow up fast; they have to, for their careers begin in the center of their youth when the rest of the world is playing games and learning to live.

December 18: We rehearse *A Midsummer Night's Dream.* I'm too old for butterflies and too young for fairies. I'm stuck in the middle—neither here not there, not new enough or old enough. As a result, I understudy both.

We have a five-minute break, and there is a mass exodus to the dressing room. We slump back in our chairs, light up cigarettes, sip cold coffee and sing along to the radio. We face ourselves in our makeup mirrors. The edge of the glass is adorned with cards from admirers, a special pair of toe shoes, good-luck charms, poems and flowers. As we make up our faces each night, we are constantly reminded of the people we love and those who love us. We need these quiet comforting symbols each night before we put ourselves on display.

The break is over. We pack ourselves up, back to the studio. We have regained the dignity that we lost by being subjected to the demands of others.

Peter and Suzanne rehearse the divertissement pas de deux from Act II. The audience is filled with small groups of tourists, and Balanchine sits cross-legged and pensive on center stage. He occasionally rises to demonstrate a correction or make a suggestion. Peter is wearing ballet slippers, bare legs, short shorts and a T-shirt. His legs look larger and more muscled in the flesh: strong, thick, solid, smooth legs. His face is disinterested. Despite his apparent unreadiness, he whips off pirouettes, beats and jumps with his predictable grace and ease.

Suzanne is in a black leotard, baggy maroon velvet sweat pants, slim blue leg warmers and shiny new white pointe shoes. Her brown hair, held up by a single clip, loosens and spreads as she dances. Her face is unpainted but glorious, a wise and beautiful face. The big blue eyes speak of her humor, her sympathy, her devotion, her romance, her experience, her suffering and her care.

She is most attentive to Balanchine, dancing for him. Peter listens but tries to maintain an aura of independence and self-composure, appearing to consider carefully and filter every remark of Balanchine's and then appearing in agreement as if it were the verbalization of his own thoughts.

Heather Watts enters. She is in pink today: a pink scarf knotted around her head, a pink leotard, pink tights, pink sweat pants, pink leg warmers, pink shoes and a pink ballet bag, each pink different from the others; textures, materials and styles all different. Her face is alive, Californian and emotional. She glows, but her entrance passes unnoticed. She has a Coke bottle. She sits at the front of the stage to jabber to whomever will listen.

The rehearsal is smooth and soon over. The company disperses. In the corner where Heather sat lies the tiny shredded debris of the label from her Coke.

December 19: Darci Kistler (our youngest star, although she is still in the corps) emerges from the elevator in a white sweat shirt decorated with cartoon images, a big smile on her face and a red lollipop in her hand. Her future is set, and we all pray she doesn't lose her priceless innocent enthusiasm.

I skidded on my bottom in the snow tonight, but the audience didn't see it. As I exited by the first wing in a flying grand jeté, I landed flat on my tail at Mr. B.'s feet. He looked down with satisfaction and sniffed. I was heartily congratulated on my perfectly placed mishap, for Mr. B. is known to like those who fall; it indicates an energy and fearlessness that is essential to excitement. I'm afraid my fall was not attributable to such lofty pursuits but just to slippery snow. It is very slippery—all those tiny rounds of paper. They are swept up after Act I into barrels. Apparently they cost $1,200 a barrel because they are fireproof.

We are a good two weeks into *Nutcracker* so the snow

has become interesting, for along with the paper pellets everything else imaginable is swept up and deposited on our heads the next day—lost earrings, dirt, bits of glass, even a wire coat hanger clunked to the ground recently. It's a dangerous business, this snow! It sticks to everything, goes in our ears, up our noses and down our throats—and it's anything but cherry-flavored!

Tonight I noticed conductor Robert Irving's amused and indulgent grin as he tried to time the music to the little Prince's pantomime. The Prince was just forging ahead regardless, and Mr. Irving was divine. The satisfaction on his face and the wink he gave when the great climax was reached simultaneously were priceless.

Darci danced the Dewdrop tonight, and I had lazily sprawled myself on a stool to watch. She smiled, glowed, jumped and twirled. As she came offstage, she confessed to me that she had been "holding back." "It was slippery, so I was afraid," she said. "You know, I feel bad if I haven't done my best." Oh, how ashamed I felt, sitting on my stool as this giving girl confessed this to me, who gives so little by comparison. Her simplicity was frightening. Why not always do one's best? And then one's best can always be better. And there I sat just enjoying myself, not doing tendus or stretching or trying at all but simply enjoying. Why do we all at times lose that simplicity, that undeviating direction, and become seemingly lazy, apathetic, even uninterested as our thoughts wander? Dancing may indeed be the most beautiful and romantic of arts, but no dreamers allowed—work is work, be it loading trucks or doing tendus. All that work is for all that beauty.

Dancing is funny sometimes. Sometimes one is so tired that no reason on earth can be found to justify why one is trying. Sometimes one's body and mind are so tired that forcing them to function seems more than is possible. Glimpses of beauty always trickle in; we are so surrounded by it that it is unavoidable, and yet . . . the forcing of oneself denies all reason. Really, we dance too much, sometimes too long, twelve hours a day. By eight o'clock when the curtain rises all we can rustle up are the steps and a remembered smile. Dancing should be joy for us; if we must force it, surely the audience can feel it.

December 20: I indulged in my first Christmas festivities last night—a late night at a friend's, wine, food, laughs and warmth. But oh, how hard it was to rise and dance today; the hangover was the least of the problems. All I wanted was more of the lazy ways.

Tonight when I stood in the corps to bow, I felt out of place, cheated to be there. And then I remembered what Balanchine always says: "If you don't like it, leave. Don't stay and complain." And yet those who stood in front of me, were they really so much more deserving of their place? Luck, chance and one man's whim can put one dancer in front of another. It is not always fair.

December 21: Classroom excitement: Mary Tyler Moore took class today, and what indiscreet star-gazers we were. We are always awestruck by stars of other media. When James Cagney visited backstage, we went wild—far more than for Rudi or Dame Margot. Al Pacino, Robert De Niro, Candice Bergen caused a real stir. If you act or sing, we are starstruck; if you only dance, well, you're just one of us.

Mary Tyler Moore's strangely short, fuzzy hair, her black leotard and leg warmers, her body and face and makeup and attitude were all on show. She was slim, worked hard, chewed gum voraciously and did every step. We were all condescendingly impressed. "Not bad" for a nondancer. Even Suzanne's eyes surveyed our newest member.

The Christmas spirit has entered the theater. Christmas lights flash in our dressing rooms, little plastic trees have been set up, Christmas carols are played, and there is a mysterious, constant flow of sustenance—champagne, fruitcake, cookies and chocolate. Our travel agent sent us a huge dark-chocolate leg from Krön. Mr. Bigelow, our company manager, introduced the offering before class to great amusement. We noted the slim elegant shape, but criticized the bent knee and pointed toe. Mr. B. sent a message that specifically the girls in "Waltz of the Flowers" should partake of the leg—he had recently complained that they lacked energy. The leg was placed outside our dressing rooms and quietly demolished. We took a special pleasure in mutilating that symbol of our existence. Some wanted toes, thighs, knees, the tendon. Unfortunately, the leg was hollow, so those who asked for bones and joints went sadly hungry!

There is a strange underground echelon developing among us of college-minded girls—older girls. They take courses, study for SATs and celebrate their test scores. Schoolbooks clutter our dressing rooms, mixing with the newspapers, programs and copies of *Vogue*. As more and more girls show interest, it is quite openly discussed within the confidential walls of the dressing room. The joy and childlike reactions to the academic world are amazing. One girl is taking a course in logic: "I've always acted on feeling and intuition. Now for the first time I'm learning how to put the two sides of a question together and judge objectively." She is thrilled and amazed at the new possibilities. She speaks of the wonderful sensation of a positive action for herself, initiated by herself. She is controlling her destiny, something totally unknown to the rest of us. We dance, but our fate and our future are entirely dependent on the strength of our bodies and the whims of others.

I've read the words of men of reason who consider physical preoccupation the lowest possible concern. The body is mortal, and yet the beauty it makes is not. Walt Whitman says our body is our soul, for what else do we have than our body to work with. But I fear Plato would disapprove of my calling!

December 22: We just voted to give the power to AGMA and our representatives to order us to stop work in two weeks if management does not budge. I'm absolutely incredulous that such a thing came to pass. Forty-nine people, less the half the New York City Ballet, showed up. No doubt the rest were sleeping or Christmas shopping. All I can feel is outrage. Once again our day-to-day existence predominates in most minds. Christmas is in three days, and the prospect of future Christmases is too far away to bother about. So forty-nine of us decided the future, or rather, the sixty absent ones decided our future.

There was a general quiet, tired, apathetic atmosphere as opposed to the previous meeting. The management offer, only slightly better and more detailed than the last proposal, was rejected, twenty-five to twenty-three. Some kids had appointments for massages and left. Then we took the strike vote: twenty-six to eighteen in favor. The disorganized, hurried procedure on the most important vote of all was appalling. We each scribbled yes or no on a piece of paper. Then a few voices cried out. Some people did not know which was which. We begged that those who voted in such ignorance speak up now, but pride kept all tongues silent. Those of us against the vote were shocked. As always, the rebellious and militant were ever-present and loud, while those who did not think that there could be a strike and did not want one were absent, never guessing that some of their peers would be deciding their future against their own wishes.

If everyone had been present, such a vote would not have come to pass. The issue to me is a moral one. Those who refuse to see it in such a light but say it is purely political and economic are protecting their moral guilt for such an action. To strike is to demand more money in our pockets (which we do indeed need, even though we are the highest-paid company in the world). In our insecure world, who is not for such a self-protective cause as each man for himself? But we are not fighting against an organization but against one man—an artist (here I use the word in total adoration and respect, as the highest label of the highest human being). Those who respond that they are not fighting Balanchine but the New York City Ballet management are attempting to allay their guilt. After all, not one of us would admit to fighting against Balanchine. But we are. He feels it as a total personal affront, and why shouldn't he? By this pathetic "majority" we have stabbed him. He was hurt, furious, outraged. He has said that he will leave and take his ballets. He has also said that we do not need more money, that a sixteen-year-old new company member should not get more money. He will care for us, but he can't pay our rent. I know I am inconsistent in my point of view, but I see both sides and hear both cries.

They say he has always dictated and had his own way with us, and we will stand for it no longer. They say he does not respect us by not sympathizing with our financial demands. How ironic that in the country he so loves, the values will destroy him. Only here does respect rest on a show of dollars. Ultimately in America the proof of love, respect, success and moral worth is money. Oh dear.

And so the choice is to stand up for ourselves, our security, our financial security, or to give second place to such values and act on respect, devotion, love and deep belief in one man. I opt for the second without hesitation. Balanchine is more important and valuable than we are individually. If personal security is our primary aim, dancing is not the career for us. It flourishes and feeds off all the qualities created by a lack of security.

The company has become big, so the money must go farther, and Balanchine has lost much of the devotion that he has earned. The twenty-five new corps dancers barely know him at all. I have been with him five years; I am the tail end of those who've had the personal contact with him essential to build the love that he needs from us, and that we need to have faith in him. The young kids cry out for themselves alone. "What has he done for me?" they ask. Many have never spoken to him. Even I know him mostly from reading about him and from watching his ballets. Balanchine has grown apart from us because of his age, his illnesses and the sheer difficulty of personal contact with so many people.

We all hear the stories of the old days when the company was small, when he taught class every day, when he personally coached and talked and lived with his dancers. That is impossible now, and time has separated him from his tools. So the affinity is lost. He has hurt himself by his growth.

He wants such a big, big wonderful company—and it has become impossible to retain its allegiance. Perhaps this is a significant symbol of a utopian dictatorship, which is what I called NYCB. Perhaps one hundred people is the maximum number possible for one man to touch and influence enough to win their faith in him.

Those who love themselves more than Balanchine have made their stand and demonstrated their lack of faith in him. They cry they have belief in him as an artist but not as their dictator. But how can one separate the two when his art can be produced only out of a state that he alone must rule? It's a pity he needs a hundred individuals as his tools rather than paintbrushes. What would have happened if Van Gogh's brushes one day had refused to be manipulated because they wanted better living conditions?

December 23: Mr. Balanchine requested a talk with the whole company. The meeting was right after class, so class was full of faces we had not seen for months and months. It felt like the old days (yes, even to me, three or four years back) when Mr. B. taught and everyone was there, dressed to kill and crowding the barres so that we had to do every exercise to the side because front and back were impossible. It really forced our turnouts! Class was an energetic blur of moving bodies. After all, "he" might walk in early, and one must be up front sweating! The barres were lined with leaning bodies in animated discussion—what would he say? —and everyone had his own prediction.

He walked in calmly and quietly and called us around him. We all shuffled on our bottoms to his feet. Peter Martins and a few senior men remained standing in the back, unable to be so childlike and submissive as we, sitting at his feet. In what corporation in a strike-threat situation would you find the secretaries and workers sitting at the feet of the boss? And then we complain that we are always considered boys and girls, not men and women—our child-like positions on the floor are self-condemning!

Would anyone dare speak back? Or offer an argument? We all hoped for it, knowing no one would risk his career so obviously. Mr. B. spoke for ten minutes in a simple, friendly way. He and Lincoln Kirstein were the heads and rulers, and their offer was final. They would simply not accept twenty-two out of a hundred and five as a majority to decide the future of New York City Ballet. If seventy out of a hundred and five voted to strike, then, "Fine, okay, I will be happy. We will go elsewhere and make a new company in a day. This is the fifth company, and we will make the sixth. We have always done so. You can go to John Clifford, Canada, Ballet Theatre, Europe—fine. I want a vote for myself, and I don't give a damn if it's illegal. Yes or no from a hundred and five!"

I'm sure at this point my stomach was not the only one that jumped when I thought he was asking for us to raise our hands right there in front of him to decide whether to end NYCB or not! He could have, and we would have responded. No one would have dared speak out or vote no.

But he did not. He told us there would be a box. "I want to know what you think, and that's all," and so ended his first talk to all of us together in at least three years. Perhaps if he had done this more often, and the younger ones knew him better—perhaps then the whole contract procedure would have been settled long ago. Now there is a mutual distrust, all because of lack of contact.

He mentioned that at our age he was starving with Diaghilev and sold his pants at the *Marché aux Puces* for food—"I don't care, sleep five together on the floor; you will be better dancers." Yes, he is of the old school; he believes suffering will make better artists. But in this day and age and society, we have outlawed such standards of living.

I feel cheated of a time of suffering such as Mr. B. had. We have had no opportunity to starve and work and live on the edge. We starve ourselves only out of neurosis. We are spoiled.

December 30: Nutcracker is drawing to a close along with the holiday season, and I'm wondering if it's all worth it—trying to live and celebrate and dance. I've been to parties, had parties, dinners, lunches and brunches; I've had discussions about life with good friends for twelve and fourteen hours at a stretch. I've laughed, cried, loved, cooked and made gifts. All such "good times" go against dancing, both physically and emotionally. I've eaten too much, drunk too much, slept too little—and enjoyed it all far too much. So

I feel physically out of shape, and worst of all, all my associations of pleasure come from people sharing, while dancing calls for a solitary, single-minded pursuit. I think my love and need of people will eventually conquer my dancing. Twelve years of solitude begs for company, and frankly I cannot see how to combine the two. If I talk, I must really talk and not say, "Now I must sleep." If I eat, I must really eat; if I drink, I must drink champagne. I cannot combine the two ways of life. But I cannot choose between them either. If only I did not love people so much, it would be easy. I think my case is not unique—every dancer encounters such choices, and always chooses dancing. One simply does not throw away twelve years of work, beauty, a job, money to pay the rent and a wonderful place in the greatest ballet company in the world.

Yesterday our dressing room became ill with laughter. We took a *New York Times* (who says we don't read?) and cut out headlines as our retaliation to management. The finished product, pasted up, looked like this:

Coping with Disaster
Do You Know the Man You've Elected
Grim speech
Ordinary People Voted Best
Economic Scene
$1 less than many expected
Worth arguing about

If you could do it all over again
Type in 20 hours
Summer jobs
You ought to be in pictures
Accused job bias   Group petitions to restore
'81 hiring prospects promising   You won't forget
the competition
Help wanted—a year of slumping spirits
Many choose wine
A powerful drama of conflict
Not in our stars but—
Volunteers coping
Watt's very wrong
Soviet invasion
Drug issues increase strongly
Group petitions to restore
Administration agrees to panel on activists' surveillance
Court delays union rulings
Feverish Farfetched and Downright Scary

We are truly the rebellious children, satisfied to make a
stand and be heard and respected, though not gaining another dollar, for the contract we will now accept is financially identical to that we rejected six or seven weeks ago!

We have accepted on the condition that we, the dancers,
will be allowed to look at the books and help with fund-
raising. I guarantee that this "compromise" will not be
exercised, but it helped us to save face.

January 3, 1981: *The Nutcracker* closes tomorrow. The theater is full of little people asking for used toe shoes and autographs. They know their time is up on the great stage, so they will take us with them. I still have autographed shoes from my days as a hoop!

Performances these days have virtually no one whose name appears in the program. Between injuries, illnesses and emergency rehearsals, there are twenty to thirty replacements at every performance. The daily schedule is a mass of substituted names. 'Tis the season for illness and injury.

Adam Lüders, known for his incredibly arched feet, tells me that not only can he not get up from the floor (a very common complaint), but his left foot is nonfunctioning, unattached and totally rebellious. We decide to cut it off and put it in formaldehyde in the museum—in the famous-parts section, next to Einstein's brain.

It has occurred to me lately that now is the pinnacle of success in our lives and anything done after we have left the New York City Ballet will be a comedown. Now we are glamorous, loved and desirable. The public loves us, socialites prize us at their parties, and we are respected everywhere simply because of our position. Stores take my checks when I say I'm in NYCB. The rich are most giving, kind and generous. We are desirable people, beautiful people. When New York City Ballet is no longer a claim, the stores will not take my checks, I will not be invited to glamorous parties or receive flowers from admirers. In the space of one day, one can lose that hold over the world and fall into the regular human condition. Who is interested in a dancer who once danced?

January 4: We just finished a truly great performance, from the dancing itself to hysterical mistakes. Today's handwritten schedule was a good three and a half feet long, with some thirty-odd replacements. The trouble started immediately. Delia went on at the last minute for an absent Renée —bowing with loose wispy hair and dangling ribbons. One girl arrived so late her replacement had been called, and they both arrived together to dance the same spot. There were tears and grimaces among the Flowers due to injuries, stomach pains and having to do a part they had never done before (they had been thrown on at the last minute). The performance was their first. Best of all, no one realized until the angels were gliding around the stage in the second act that there was no lead for "Spanish"—the very next dance. Heather grabbed the costume, and with soft ballet shoes, not a scrap of makeup and a crooked headpiece, she improvised her way through, kicking her partner at every opportunity while he tried desperately to predict her next move.

I've never seen the wings so full of eager faces—people piled high on shoulders and stools to get a look at the show. Even Mr. B. managed a grin. And yes, there was some wonderful dancing to make up for the craziness. Darci danced with Peter Martins for the first time, and it was truly heartwarming. She even squeezed a good-natured grin out of him with her eager smile. The age difference was lovely, and Darci triumphed. We all cheered madly. Even after thirty-nine performances, *The Nutcracker* can still excite us. And to sum it all up along personal lines, it was all so beautiful and such fun that my crazed introspection is buried in the grave of unimportance that it merits!

". . . am I not their doctor? In me, through me, all the secrets of medicine are secretly bartered for all the secrets of the dancer. They call me in for everything and anything. Sprains, spots, vapors, heartaches, the various accidents of their profession (and those substantial accidents so easily inferred in a career so active and unsettled)—and all their mysterious ailments, every jealousy, whether artistic or emotional; even dreams."

—Antoine de Saint-Exupéry, The Wisdom of the Sands

January 5: I'm truly sad today. I'm twenty-two, and feel that my career is at a standstill. For eleven or twelve years it has moved forward, and now it is stagnating and going nowhere. What can I feel but at some sort of ending? Twenty-two and my career, a big section of my life, feels over. I suppose I should be happy I am still young enough to begin again, but I've no money, no lover, no future I can see, only the same ballets, season after season. I am not alone. I'm sure forty other girls feel the same at times. But on we go day by day, rehearsing the same ballets. When the curtain goes up, there is fifteen minutes of joy and pleasure; the next day the same thing happens all over again.

January 6: I have just come from class. Damn, damn that mirror, showing shamelessly every New Year pound, every bite of fruitcake and glass of champagne. It's just so hard to "feel" oneself, the muscle control, when that wretched mirror reflects back an image, not a sensation. A cold, one-dimensional glass image doesn't help progress. This dreaded disease of mirror-gazing must be eradicated. One becomes hypnotized in horror. I compare notes and find some solace.

I stand on the side watching the steps go by, pretending to myself that watching is interesting, knowing full well that I'm searching out excuses for being an audience and not a performer. I look in amazement at each sweating body—trying, failing and trying again—and I wonder where on earth they find the strength of mind to continue. And so I talk and talk to myself, knowing that I'm simply avoiding the real issue at hand—to get out there and try myself.

I proceed to list all my positive attributes as a human being, since I obviously have none as a dancer. I run a quick scan of my life and accomplishments through my brain, picking out all the good. It doesn't help. If one is a lousy dancer at any given moment of the night or day, there is no help or sympathy to be found in one's "former" talent of yesterday. One must resort to human values, but dancers do not train to be "human," only to dance—so our self-worth relies totally on dancing and the values that apply. What else is there? There is the example of the good survivors, those who bounce back over and over. They have an outside life and outside interests, so when dancing fails, they can keep themselves occupied in a nondestructive way and wait for the will to dance to emerge again of its own accord, because, as I know so well, when one's entire being finds no pleasure or value in dancing, one's body will not dance. It will go painfully through the motions, but who would want to look at it? Even the muscles react differently when internal conflict takes over. There is no faking of the will to dance; it is not something within our control—our conscious control. Forcing such an act is absurd and unproductive, as any dancer will tell you.

What a jagged day—one hour of rehearsal, one hour off. I escape the claustrophobia of the theater every hour, but by the time I'm dressed and settled in the coffee shop, I check the clock and have to leave. We rehearse the *Stars and Stripes* finale for the hundredth time. The same thing I danced four and a half years ago. This reeks of stagnation to me.

January 7: The day:
    10:15 A.M.: Slowly the dressing room fills up, lights are turned on, the radio station is adjusted, snowy boots are pulled off and layers of coats and sweaters are thrown down, hot coffees are opened and cigarettes are lit. There is small talk about the snow—"It won't last, but how beautiful"; about the article in the paper on our contract settlement— "They called it 'comfortable,' what a joke."
    10:45: We all make it to class, which has already begun

on pliés. Not an inch of flesh is showing: layer upon layer of sweaters, sweat pants, warmers, scarfs and shoes. People lean on the barres catching their breath, breathing hard and holding on for support. They are stretching, kneeling, sitting and leaning. Bodies are sprawled in splits, side splits and front splits. Legs are pulled and pushed and massaged. Legs are around the necks and above the shoulders; legs are shaken loose, realigned and retightened.

Just a few people stand unsupported in the center of the studio, dancing, balancing, turning and trying.

Balanchine enters, walks across the huge studio and sits on a chair dead-center. He cocks his head back, crosses his legs and awaits the show.

He has no need to wait. Sweaters are ripped off, legs become visible, hard shoes are softened and no one sits on the floor. The group in the center triples in size. Everyone is smiling and trying to push up front. The girls end their jump sequence under Mr. B.'s nose. He shifts again. Faces are so eager that it has all the appearance of an audition—yet we are all hired. So for an hour we work, wake up and discover the day's pains and injuries.

11:45: We reconvene in the dressing room, more awake, with wet clothes and flushed faces. We read the paper, sew shoes, discuss the recent marriage of a friend.

12:00: First rehearsal on stage, beginning as usual with the finale (so that those who are only in that can leave), then taking it from the beginning. The small girls end their regiment with one girl crumpled on the floor in tears. A few people ask her what is wrong; others just pass by with a glance. We know the problem—a pain somewhere in the body, mimicking a pain in the head. Must I be out? I can't be out! What is the best thing to do? She gets up and continues dancing. The girls have all taken class and are serious and ready to begin dancing. The boys, on the other hand, are mostly direct from bed, relaxed, smiling, joking and full of boyish beans. I wonder about this class-taking business. Bodies are well wrapped and more than one neck is cuddled in leg warmers. Colds, coughs, sniffles and headaches are going around.

12:30: We finish and pile into the elevator, sweating and puffing. An outsider arrives, exclaiming, "My God, girls, it's only twelve-thirty, and look at you!"

I'm asked if I would like to be out of *Stars*. "I don't know any more. I like performing it, but hate rehearsing it." "Oh, I just wondered if anyone liked this ballet." We laugh.

No doubt the ballet could have used more rehearsal time —it always can—but the schedule is already loaded with overlapping rehearsals. Someone complains that they have to be at three rehearsals at the same time: "I think I'll compromise and go to lunch!"

2:00: Rehearsal with Balanchine. All the warm layers are removed again. He arrives very late. The atmosphere is tense; silence is broken by ripples of quiet and shy laughter. He sits on a chair, his head cocked to one side, then to the back, constantly sniffing.

"All my Danish pastries are out," he says, referring to all our injured Danish dancers.

Heather Watts and Victor Castelli rehearse *Agon* pas de deux. Heather's hair is neither up nor down and her face is sleepy, but her body is responsive. She wears an odd leotard, odd blue sweat pants, and odd old toe shoes. There are soft-spoken defenses: "I'm so tired," "I'm not even awake." The dancers offer all questions in the form of suggestions, meanwhile watching Mr. B.'s face for any sign. He is talkative and amiable and offers help and grunts of approval. Where to put the legs: "It doesn't have to be so low," "Don't go to the knee . . ." He receives "Ohs" and experiments in response; he continues: ". . . like *Four Temperaments.*" People laugh at his analogy. He always makes ironic references to his other ballets. "Yes, yes, that's right." There is a sigh of relief; this is his highest praise.

"Bend it . . . one, two, three, four, five, six, in tempo. Don't do anything, wait the eight . . . All right, and one, two, three, four, five, six, seven, eight, one and two and three, slowly . . . Now move. Don't do too much, we don't want that, and one, two, three, four, five, six, seven, eight . . . Now one and two and three and you're here, your hand goes down, you wait and one, two, three, four, five, six, seven, and eight, one and two and three . . . That's right." They made it through the sore spot.

The doorway to the studio has slowly filled up with passers-by—stagehands, photographers, children and dancers.

"Your leg should be forward . . . You do *dadadaditum*—you just peel her down . . . Go again . . . Thaaat's right!"

He looks pleased. "You could do this." Balanchine is out of his chair in a jiffy and takes over from Victor. As always, Mr. B. completes the sequence with the greatest of ease. Victor grins and makes the gesture as if to say, "It's all yours, you won the audition!" Victor takes over again and tries to imitate Balanchine's finesse. He succeeds with twice the effort. Mr. B. flings his arms up: "You see how easy it is!"

Heather and Victor repeat the lunge, to make sure their success was not just luck. They continue. "That's right—it's like modern—bang!" They hit on a lucky streak, and all goes smoothly for at least forty seconds.

"Take her hand, bring her in, that's right . . . *dadida* . . . Now go, quickly—bang! Now go again, slowly *da da da dum,* that's right—the longer you take the better; where are you rushing to? We're not going anywhere, are we?"

"Here it's like *Sleeping Beauty,* you know." There are more giggles.

The pas de deux is over, and the dancers breathe a sigh of relief. Mr. B. looks pleased, and the three leave the studio.

Now two hours off to reenter the real world, but with far less desperation than yesterday. How strange—the theater is a jail one day and a heaven the next!

Another rehearsal break. Two of our college-bound

dancers discuss their Monday Dante course. The dressing room has never heard such talk—of religion, John the Baptist, Beatrice, Vergil and times B.C. All are silent, sewing ribbons on toe shoes with open, curious ears.

The day, continued:

8:00: The performance begins. So good to hear other music again. *The Nutcracker* forty times does get tedious. Ah, to be rid of sugar and spice and dance to Stravinsky in leotards. Between ballets we laugh, confess our faux pas on stage and discuss the board of directors. "These are really powerful, classy people." All ears are pricked again and questions flow forth. The usual jokes about the rich and the poor. (We are the poor.)

10:15: Exactly twelve hours after the dressing-room lights were switched on and the morning coffee was sipped, we finish the day with a grand finale. A basket of crudités and two bottles of white wine await us in the dressing room, left over from a party out front.

Warmed by the wine and the thought of bed, we all bundle up to go home. A howling blast of wind meets us in the real world. The snow looks even more beautiful through my blurred eyes, still filled with baby oil from a too-rapid makeup removal.

I stop at a deli for a salad—no food at home—and go straight to bed to nurse my aching feet (when cold, my left foot will not bend beyond two degrees off the perpendicular—not a pretty sight). The day is over.

I had a thought tonight while watching the boys' regiment in *Stars*. They all looked so terrifically and appealingly young—younger than their years. It was not only their soldier dress; their faces all looking straight ahead into the black hole of the audience were so vulnerable, so unknowing, and so open. I suppose it is the eagerness to please the audience each night that prevents them from growing old and accepting; that keeps them like children.

January 8: We had a crazed rehearsal today. Two girls were injured and dropped out in the middle. We all wonder where the "understudies" have gone. It turns out they are all in it already, so we must resort to old girls.

"Where is so-and-so?"

"Oh, she's out."

"Out? She hasn't danced for five weeks; she's on vacation."

Mr. B. was in one of his most pensive and dejected moods. "It's not right. It's never been right and never will be right!"

And so there I sat in the coffee shop filled with despair in my lonely dancer's life. An old dignified man sat nearby. I could feel his eyes upon me and awaited a word. I received not a word but a tirade. He had seen Nijinsky, Lifar, the Ballets Russes in Paris, the Kirov in Leningrad; every dancer, choreographer and composer of the thirties and forties was vivid in his mind. "No, no," he said sadly, "it is not the same any more. It is dying. Where is all that wonder of *Schéhérazade* and *Daphnis et Chloé* and of the perfect *Swan Lake*?"

His words had little effect on my self-pity, but his eyes did. I had evoked his memories by the fact that I was a dancer, by the beauty that my profession suggested to him. I felt historic—a member of the remaining family of this beautiful art and tradition. I was truly shamed from my small world of self-pity and given a sense of great importance.

During the course of the day, more girls had to take to their sickbeds. At six o'clock, a ballet was canceled and the program altered. Whether because of relief at not having to dance or merely from the simple joy of a change in the routine, many faces glowed at the cancellation.

Thereupon I took thought of the dancers, courtesans, and singers in my city. They had litters of silver made for them and when they ventured forth therein, they bade runners go before them to announce their coming and cause the crowd to gather. Then when the applause of the multitude had wrought agreeably on their nerves and roused them from their fragile slumbers, they would draw aside the silken veils before their faces and deign to pander to the desire of the crowd by yielding glimpses of their pale beauty. Demurely they smiled, while the runners did their task with all their might, for they were flogged at nightfall if the crowd had not forced the dancers' modesty by the insistence of its desire.

—*Antoine de Saint-Exupéry,* The Wisdom of the Sands

You have done an admirable thing,
Through spirit, with little substance,
You have created a woman more beautiful than the
    rose—
One whose soul I desired to hold more than my own—
You radiate your sex, its warmth, its style—I fear that I
    may never capture a more perfect kiss.
But such a will is too strong and devours much of
    life.
Because of you I have felt and strived for rich passion.
    But you are your own mistress.

So he wrote to Isabelle, her poet—a dancer. She moved
on from the Duke to gentleness, tenderness, sweetness and
poetry. Not a day passed without a word, a thought, put
on paper for her. And all that remains now are those scribbled notes.

They lived out every whim of romantic love—secret
meetings, intrigue and grand plans for a life together. They
were playmates, accomplices. They would conquer the
world together, so great was their youth, their beauty, their
energy. Isabelle learned innocence again through their tenderness.

Their love was recorded and preserved and predicted. It
predicted its own demise. Such a romance could not last for
them. They were dancers. They must work. The reality of
their work in the theater went ignored and unexamined

while they continued to dream. "I am happier with you than with any other I know or have ever known—or could dream of knowing."

All the while their careers moved forward. She competed with forty other girls, he with twenty-four other boys. He soared ahead while Isabelle stayed behind. They were not prepared for this separation. They had not talked of such a possibility. Their love was born in candlelight, not at the ballet barre. They had not discussed their lives of tomorrow, only their immortality.

And so his poems ceased as his career took flight. His energy was turned to sweat, not thought. Isabelle and her poet were confronted by reality, and it hit as suddenly and as abruptly as a cement wall. Their romance cracked. There was no time any more for planning and dreaming. And so they went their separate ways.

> *Others might dance, others bend their fresh and lively minds upon the pleasure in hand!*
>
> — *Thomas Mann, "Tonio Kröger"*

January 9: Tonight I watched several girls who were my peers and many younger race ahead to stardom on the big stage. As the curtain rose, all my friends became goddesses, and I felt alone and mortal. I forced myself to face the fact that I refuse to face every day; I am going nowhere. I can stay and stagnate, or I must change my life. I really find it grossly unfair to have to feel such impending doom at my age.

I had a nightmare last night about Balanchine. He told me I danced like a Biafran—no substance. I awoke with a great fear and knew I must go and dance before him. My faith in dancing is gone, but my faith in life cannot be, or else I would not be here writing this page.

January 10: "How are the mighty fallen." I dread the theater, where I have no strength anymore to put on a happy visage. I have found one never has so many friends as when one is sad. Don't they know that every sympathetic look or word is like a dagger and makes my stomach bleed? Can I not admit defeat? Certainly not to them who are still aiming for success.

I know I must leave. My direction and view must change, and yet . . . yet forever I ask why and how and whence comes this deep pain. I search for its cause, its last and most basic cause. Is it the competition? Is it the solitude? Is it the physical pain, fatigue and strain? Is it my position in the corps, where I am unneeded and seemingly unnoticed? Do I affect my success, or do they—the management? Was it my fate that through the whim of others I have ended here like this? Can I induce my fate to be guided differently?

Must the source of my education, my energy, my dedication and my adoration also be that which teaches me pain and tears? Is this a lesson of love that I contemplate too readily, too frequently and too deeply? Does dancing force too great a humility upon me so that I cannot endure the judgment and advice even of those who know?

January 11: It is four-twenty, between matinee and evening. The stage is dimly lit, and not a soul is around. The curtain is up, and one solitary pair of legs perched in the second ring is the only sign of life. Then the music begins. Our pianist Gordon Boelzner is rehearsing *Tchaikovsky Piano Concerto No. 2* in the orchestra pit. The gorgeous sounds rise and fill the huge empty space. He messes up, stops and starts again. This is special. An empty theater is like a church. I am moved by the music.

The more I watch from the wings the creation on stage every night, the less reason I find to do my own tendus. What could I possibly add? It is perfect. To think that for three hours every night such offerings of beauty are made on stage while we sew our ribbons, laugh and listen to WABC.

I have the fear of failure, so now I pretend to have chosen it, just to placate myself a little. I'd like to think that my awe, admiration and adoration for great dancing and great ballets has predestined me to fail in attempting it myself. I can only hope that my failure has such a lofty source. I'll never know; no one will.

All the kids around here talk to Mr. B. about the weather, their toe shoes and their vacations. I've not only always thought this inappropriate but quite a shocking, insensitive waste of a great man's time—and yet he apparently enjoys it and encourages it.

Five years ago, when I was first in the company, when I was first behind the big gold curtain at the New York State Theater, I saw strange things every day. I saw pretty, flirty ballet girls in pretty, flirty, flimsy ballet clothes talking to Balanchine. I heard things like: " . . . and my left toe shoe always gets softer than my right—I just don't know what to do," and "They said it would rain, but it hasn't, has it?" and "Mr. B., how can I improve my hairdo?" And as if that wasn't strange enough, he answered them. Not only did he reply, he replied in an altogether shocking way—he was genuinely interested and attentive.

I could not fathom this. It was absurd to me. How could the man who made *Serenade* and *Apollo* in the beginning, *Union Jack* and *Vienna Waltzes* a few years ago and *Violin Concerto* in between talk about the weather? I could not understand it. I was sure that his mind traveled on different planes than ours.

Here is one dancer who cannot talk to Balanchine about the weather. I decided a while back that awe and fear was not good for my dancing—I shook when he looked at me. I attempted to dispel this by talking to him about it. He said, "But, dear, why? I'm just like you or any other man." Then we talked of Paris and champagne. For a few moments afterwards I almost believed he was like me—until I went on stage and watched *Concerto Barocco.* All my fear returned a hundredfold. He was kidding me. He is definitely not like me.

When the curtain falls on *Concerto Barocco,* ten girls in white are on their knees. They are plunged for a minute into total blackness as the first gold threads of the curtain touch the stage. As the lighting is readjusted, they struggle with no small effort to rise and back up for the bows. They have about ten seconds before the curtain re-exposes them. In that time, skirts are recentered, escaped ribbons are captured, little streams of sweat are redirected away from the eyes. The principal girls have farther to travel with their protesting bodies—all the way to the wings. More often than not they limp.

The curtain swoops up as the last stray wisps of hair are brushed back. The girls pop up with lightning speed from their inelegant positions, usually holding their feet. (We talk to our feet, we apologize to our feet.) By the time the first bows are over, the girls have regained most of their consciousness. They return from that breathless state that demands a withdrawal from reality. More often than not a verbal barrage of great wit and irony will emerge as the sacred silence that exists while we are dancing is broken. I cannot help feeling that the often defensive jesting and self-mockery are the direct result of having just bared one's work, one's quality, one's care. On stage there is no deception. The body and soul are bared when flesh is combined with movement.

The oral onslaught has the effect of removing the profundity of the ballet. This is necessary. "It was soooo slow; how could he?" "Shit, I made so many mistakes. Was Rosemary watching?" "I've never never danced so badly, I'm in shock!" There is also the not-too-infrequent "Wow, that was fun!" But however well or badly the performance went, it cannot be expressed adequately. We are forever resorting to repetition and magnificent exaggerations in the attempt to explain. No one can. The act of dancing refuses to be adequately described on any level. It is a silent world.

The most telling signs of the performance are visual. Girls limping offstage in tears, bodies laid out flat in the wings, chests heaving and gasping for breath, soaked skin, costumes and hair. It is also possible, on occasion, to witness a peaceful smile of supreme joy.

As the curtain rises on the last bow, the backstage area, full of spectators before, has cleared. There is nothing more of importance to see. So as six thousand hands are applauding, there is a strangely ironic feeling of loneliness and desertion on stage.

The ballet is over and remains only momentarily in the minds of anyone backstage. There is another ballet to come. The girls grab for their hairpins and quickly and expertly rip their long hair out of its secure little buns. The next ballet is bound to require a different do. As the dancers leave the stage, the stagehands leap with well-practiced dexterity from their poker game and begin pulling, tugging and moving the scenery on and off the stage. Ropes go up, wings come down and sweaty tissues are gathered from their far-flung positions in the stage lights.

Meanwhile the girls have grabbed their leg warmers from the floor and are huddled in a bunch waiting for the elevator. Stripping begins, leotards are unpinned (they are literally pinned and sewn onto us). Toe shoes cannot be ripped off quickly enough, and they must often undergo a brutal beating on the nearest wall. They have rarely served us well enough. We tend to be grossly unfair, in fact. It is not enough that in the space of five minutes they have been transformed from peachy shiny satin into dirty wet deformities; we also insist on pouring out an onslaught of criticism that would destroy any being capable of response. The speeches we give ourselves vicariously through our toe shoes are harsh, very harsh, and positively relentless.

We then turn to our feet. We inspect them for blood, blisters and any new development of old injuries. As the feet slowly regain their original human form, there are some excruciating moments. As the muscles, ligaments and bones search themselves out, the intensity of the quick change usually evokes loud and garbled moans. Bodies are hurriedly crushed into the elevator as the crucial minutes whiz by before the next ballet. There is lots to do. Upon arrival in the dressing room, bodies are flung on the beds, Coke cans are opened and drained, and faces are examined at close range for smudged mascara and loose lashes. Hair is fixed for the next ballet and makeup is retouched amid an outburst of energy and relief. It is the energy born of release from the binding rules and discipline of dancing. The humor level is high; we need it in order to continue when our bodies are in protest.

Meanwhile, as I sometimes remind myself, the audience has drained a glass of champagne and is gaily shuffling back to its seats, full of anticipation for the next ballet.

January 13: As I was warming up tonight, a stagehand was gallivanting around the barre. I put him to the test: "Stand up in first position—heels together, toes pointed east-west in a straight line, bottom in, back flat, knees straight, head held high, eyes up to heaven, arms rounded and fingers separated and alive but not tense . . . " He collapsed in a breathless gasp of laughter. I told him that was just the beginning; he hadn't even moved yet.

"You must really love this dancing to bash your body around like that," he said. I said nothing.

The evening performance of *Square Dance* is over. My face is beet-red under my layers of powder, sweat drips on the floor, my right side has a stitch in it, and I feel rather nauseated. It's a hard ballet, but there were some wonderful moments. I see other dancers come offstage out of graceful movements into an agonized limping. A friend told me that he couldn't walk home last night because his hip was in a nervous spasm, but he had given a rare performance. So it's all worth it in the end. It has to be, or why would we get up every morning and limp to the barre again?

We have a petition—not for better hours or longer lunch breaks but for better toe shoes. The standard has wavered significantly in the past year. Our complaints: (1) lumpy boxes; (2) erratic pairing; (3) huge pleats where the satin meets the shank. We have small but specialized complaints! We are also disputing whether to demand that our "makers" not die on us—our feet cannot stand the change!

I've suggested that we have no glamorous social side to our lives. That's not quite true. I've been to some parties for the New York City Ballet that will never be equaled. I'm sorry to say they were never in New York. During our six months of repertory in New York, there are no parties. But on tour we more than make up for it. In Copenhagen there were ten parties in ten days; we could barely dance each day after a night out that ended only a few hours earlier. We love it, and spirits are always at their highest. There are buffets of caviar, salmon, cheese, fruits, breads, pasta; there are endless lengths of rare filet mignon and endless champagne; there is live music and dancing into the small hours. Oh, we have grand times indeed!

Never will I forget the party in Paris. Which wine, the waiter asked us, red or white? And a bottle was handed to each of us. What style! The beauty and pride of the chefs responsible for these feasts can never be appreciated enough, and I doubt that any band of people could be more self-indulgent or merrier than NYCB at a feast!

One treat I could single out is the hospitality of Mr. and

Mrs. Leonard Davis of Palm Beach, Florida. Every year they open their house and pool to us for every day of our stay, and then give us a party on closing night. We are treated like kings and queens. The luncheon buffet changes daily—huge salads, roasted chicken or maybe a roast beef, bottomless iced bowls of shrimp and crab claws, breads, muffins, strawberries and an open bar with every kind of hard and soft drink imaginable. During the party at night under the stars, kids hold champagne glasses in the heated outdoor pool while playing volleyball and ducking one another. A band plays requests, and couples waltz, polka and jazz-dance around the pool edge. Food hot and cold, sweet and sour, flows endlessly, along with champagne, and there is a dessert table to boggle the most critical eye—cakes, pies, ice cream, brownies, soufflés, fruit. Such occasional treats and memories make all aches and pains seem less than significant. They positively disappear!

I will find out one day if it's true what I think: that life begins and ends in the mind and soul, and that dancing is a deterrent from such a life. Escapism? I don't know—I will have to find out. I will also see if I can be as desirable to the world not as an enigmatic nymph but as a plebeian.

January 15: My rebellion seems to have ended. I'm back at the barre—everything is the same yet somehow different. I'm amazed that I can still plié and tendu; turning is a phenomenon. My thoughts and emotions took me so far away from that daily routine that the shock of returning to it is amazing. The steps are the same, but I am not the same. I've been tortured, or rather I tortured myself.

Yes, I'm back, but . . . the thoughts have not left.

Despite myself I enjoy the rehearsal of *Raymonda Variations,* enjoy moving my body to the music. Then something shouts out, "But it's not supposed to feel good"—and the old conflict is back. I love all the beauty and movement but hate the life. My complaint is as old as classical dancing and as common as a cold.

There are two kinds of dancers—those who live by choice in the theater day and night and every hour in between, and the "minimums," who are there five minutes before a rehearsal or performance and flee five minutes after. The theater is their job and only a part of their life; they try to integrate it into an outside life by giving only what is required. I've always been one of the first group, dedicating my life and love and energy to the theater, and now it brings pain and dissatisfaction.

January 18: Today is my birthday. I'm twenty-three years old, and I think I've discovered my problem—not the cure, but the problem. It is not dancing that has been making me miserable, it is what dancing does not allow that I've missed. For the first time in weeks I sleep only a few hours and awaken alive and full of thoughts.

Not long ago I went to a party full of strangers—columnists, doctors, bankers, models and some do-nothings. There was a crowd in smoke-filled little rooms with endless liquor and cigarettes and marijuana. I found all the talk empty, not worth spending time on.

Slowly the barrier was broken down. I was asked to help in the kitchen—I was approved of. As the evening went on, I was the subject of many questions and comments: "What do you do, dance?" "It means a lot to you, I can tell." At this point such presumption on the part of a stranger made me burst into tears. Fortunately everyone was too occupied to notice. I replied, "Well, it's my life," and realized how proud I was to say so. A sexy young man paid no attention to me until later; then he announced, "What you do is famous—your work. Gee, it sounds weird to call dancing for Balanchine work." So I decided his previous avoidance was due to a certain awe and respect. I felt better and better. They appreciated me as a dancer, and I was all too proud to be one.

I am starved for people, life, thoughts, conversation, alternatives to my NYCB world. I need only a few hours out in the real world to return joyful and by choice to my tendus. But I must have that choice, I absolutely must. I realize I enjoy my hard-earned fame as a "ballerina," and that fame and appreciation comes only from "normal" people. We dancers are too busy and too blind to appreciate one another or ourselves.

In the New York City Ballet I am one of seventy girls

like me. Outside I'm one of seventy in the whole world—
I need that kind of appreciation for my uniqueness. And
so for the first time in a long while I feel inspired to
dance today, on no sleep, lots of red wine, cigarettes and
no food.

On with the dance! Don't let them make too much of the funeral
rites, don't let them pay too much respect to such a simple fact
as death—but without this simple fact, there would never
have been either architecture, or painting, sculpture,
or music, poetry or any other art.

— *Thomas Mann,* The Magic Mountain

My toes are bloody and aching and don't point. My hips
are swollen from too much stretching. I wouldn't mind
losing three pounds, but even that for once seems unimportant. I managed to do a barre, blocking out all thoughts and
joking. I escape my misery periodically by kidding with
friends, going to Bergman movies, satirizing myself, getting
lots of sleep, but it always returns.

I don't know if dancing is the cause of it, but my dancing
suffers the most. I've only ever danced to express my joy
in life and the beauty I sense in life, so now with no joy
and no beauty, I've no reason to point my toes. Everyone
keeps telling me the same thing, "If you had a lover . . . "
Well, I don't, I won't, and I cannot induce such a state of
love.

As happens, I'm more madly in love than ever, but it's

very one-sided. No one knows about it. My stomach is overflowing with unclaimed love, but I'm not in a fit state to seduce anyone. I've done it before, but it doesn't last. I never used to care about the idea of the eternal or the immortal or even what is constant for this life. I was too busy, too full of comings and goings. But now my only concern is to find a truth, something or someone that is constant.

I've never felt so numb on stage as I did this afternoon. When I remembered, I tried to evoke that spirit of joy that always overtook me when I was younger and more innocent. But most of the time I was in a state of shock, shock that I could be so afraid of being out there. I felt I had no place there and nothing to offer. Thank God I was surrounded! Never before have I felt so empty on stage.

I really think I'll have to be sick next week. How can I go out on that stage and be so numb again? The thought makes me tremble. The eternal struggle—to give in to one's weakness, or disregard it and forge ahead. I always chose the second, and the weaknesses vanished. Now they have emerged stronger than ever.

I live haunted and tempted by life—life after ballet. Am I wrong? Is this "life" I imagine a fantasy? Is it, as Balanchine told me, "All the same, all the same, dear, everywhere." Perhaps I must leave if only to learn that it is the same everywhere, and that the answer lies in New York City Ballet as much as anywhere on earth.

Backstage: I'm warming up. It is 2:05 and the stage manager has told the conductor to go to the pit. The ballet is *Scotch Symphony*. Suddenly there is a cry—a girl is missing. A costume hangs unclaimed in the green room. Panic. Rosemary grabs an understudy as she leaves the theater. They cut another girl from the opening section, and the understudy puts on the costume—soft shoes, no makeup, one clip to hold her wispy hair. Rosemary tells her every step from the wings. The smiles and giggles on stage increase. Later another dancer tells us that once he had just finished a huge spaghetti dinner washed down with beer when, at eight o'clock, the phone rang. He was to dance the lead in *Scotch Symphony* in five minutes. He grabbed a cab, put on the costume in the elevator, makeup in the wings. The ballet began at 8:15. "It was good, lots of energy, but my stomach felt awful."

A young dancer runs up white and panicked. The computer has gone wrong: "My paycheck should be $175, and it is for $380." Smiles spread on everyone's face; she has been promoted. But she remains unconvinced: "Oh no, the company needs money for toe shoes." How delightful, how refreshing!

I've been to two wild parties recently, both very interesting confrontations with the real world. At one I was approached with "I like your ballerina aura." "What do you mean?" "The pink eye shadow and all." It just goes to show, ideas about a ballerina are unpredictable!

At the second I was discussing dancing with a doctor when suddenly he stopped. "I don't think I want to know you any more. I don't want my image of dancers ruined." I was hurt and became even more the dancer, though I secretly understand his complaint. I'd rather not know either.

January 21: Life is beautiful, dancing is beautiful, *Raymonda* is hard, sweet, pink and very ballerina. The music sings out, the stage is big, and my feet point once again. The weather is warmer, the sun pours down, and life is good. Perhaps my sadness was simply introverted energy; the energy I now have to dance was unused on my free nights.

Performance over. I messed up, and horror filled what was joy. *Raymonda* was so pretty, and I messed up one tiny step. Never will I understand the relationship of mind and body, for my mind was the mess-up. What causes disconnection when unison is the aim, I'll never know.

I just received a phone call. What a lovely distraction! I found myself talking about the performance, describing our pink tutus and our helicopter headpieces that send all the stagehands into hysterics, talking about *Raymonda* and the history of the ballet; and my sweet listener told me about the Iranian hostages. So we shared our separate knowledges.

My life on the stage is nothing. What holds me there? Suzanne Farrell, Balanchine and now little Darci—to watch her concentration, her beautiful pure body, her young face, her eagerness, her love, her care, her work, her smile. But I deny myself. While my love goes out to them, I negate myself. I cannot do a step in earnest after witnessing such beauty. I remember the *Meditation* pas de deux last season. Suzanne and Jacques d'Amboise danced. It was choreographed for them—no one else has ever danced it. Tchaikovsky, the violin and loose hair.

The man is alone on stage, kneeling and curled. The woman enters, loves him and then leaves. I felt I was intruding upon their privacy as I stood in the second wing watching. Mr. B. was standing in the front wing, his right elbow propped up on the back frame of the velvet drop. Jacques is no longer young. Every time he dances it could be the last. Suzanne is more frequently injured.

But how they danced! Her hair is down, soft and caressing. His hair is black and stiffened. He is in black; she is in white. It is beautiful, passionate, intense, touching. The emotions are not new, yet the two on the stage seem to create them for the first time. They need them to tell their story. They dance with a conviction that silences one.

The applause thunders down. They bow and the curtain is lowered. She apologizes. She does not feel well tonight. Is he all right? They bow again. The curtain drops again. Balanchine shifts and crosses the stage alone and leaves the theater.

Suzanne and Jacques are reprimanded: "Offstage now, clear please!" The curtain rises on the next pas de deux. The air is heavy with sentiment. No one has said a word. The sounds of the dance were of violins and applause. It is over, leaving only the feeling in the pit of my stomach that something momentous has just happened.

January 22: Rehearsal runs over; the next rehearsal must be canceled. Balanchine is working on Darci. She is blond, thin, tiny and so young. He is old, gray; he squints and arches his head upward to make her analyze herself. He rises and jumps around, showing her where to go, how to do it. "Where did you learn that? Did you go somewhere?"

He is already fearful and suspicious that she will desert him and go to another for help. She assures him that no one taught her, she just did it alone. She has taught herself. He will change it.

All eyes focus on the two, moving from Darci to Balanchine, from Balanchine to Darci. Everyone wants to know what he thinks of her every step. The eyes flit back and forth, back and forth, trying to correlate and imagine their two minds. It is romantic, Darci at sixteen, Balanchine at seventy-six, coaching. It is beautiful to see.

Such daily occurrences make me afraid to leave. This theater holds great things if one has the courage to see them. Do I? I just don't know.

My ankle aches and reminds me that I too must dance.

I visit Marika, our therapist-in-residence; she has a tiny room about six feet by ten feet with a hospital bed, a sink, ice packs, mustard plasters and a scale—who dares get on that! She also has a sound machine. This consists of a spatula-like apparatus connected to a little humming machine covered with dials, numbers and flashing red lights. Electricity is sent through the metal spatula where it hits a crystal, which vibrates and sends out sound waves in the form of heat through the skin and deep into the muscle. This aids healing. In action it feels like a million tiny pinpricks.

I knock on the door. The room is without its owner but full of sprawled, aching bodies. One boy on the bed is lifting ankle weights in every possible position. A tiny girl is flat on the floor resting, awaiting Marika's instructions. Another is seated. I climb over the bodies and perch on a stool by the sink to wait.

It is six-thirty. Performance begins at eight. I sit at my "place" in the dressing room, my left foot on a chair with an ice pack tied on with a black leg warmer (my aching ankle has been diagnosed as a chronic sprain). In front of me are coffee, Tab, salad, chicken noodle soup and a bran muffin. I pick at my deli smorgasbord while sewing ribbons on my toe shoes for tonight. I can freeze my ankle for only fifteen minutes; then I must thoroughly warm it up so as to be able to move it at all. Then, after the performance, another ice pack.

And so *Raymonda* begins. It is Adam Lüders' first. As I stand in third wing, a soloist tendues and prepares to run on stage, her body ready and vibrating with anticipation. She listens for the first note—it's not her music! It is the male variation, completely out of order. Adam literally brisés from the barre backstage to reach the stage, and comes out triumphant. As a result, no one knows what the conductor will produce next. Three girls line up in the wings, each waiting for her rightful call. The crowning note: after the performance the conductor tells Adam how well he has done, still totally oblivious of his own mistake. We all let him remain in his blissful ignorance.

To my surprise, I had a good time, a really good time. Suddenly the music was fast and bright. Energy vibrated in every body and face, and the steps became the means to an end. Joy, lights and beauty once again filled me totally for a few moments, but I was left afterwards once again questioning. When the good and the bad begin to balance each other out, decisions are impossible. I feel like Hamlet: to stay or not to stay, that is my question.

January 23: It is five o'clock Friday, always the hardest time of the week and made doubly so today by a good two and a half hours of *Serenade* and *Tchaikovsky Piano Concerto No. 2* with Mr. B. I wish I could transmit on paper the fatigue, which is more emotional than physical. I am dumb with it. No thought lasts more than a second. My mind skips jaggedly around, and my body wants to sag in place. I hope that food will revive me. After all, that was only rehearsal; tonight we perform the ballets.

I try to order my mind and shame my fatigue. Does this state have any value, or is it purely a result? I fear it is the second. As usual, I resent and feel guilty about the mindless state physical exertion gives birth to. Now more than ever it is obvious that our roles as dancers are to be purely instruments in an artwork. I suppose what I feel is simply the loss of self-control.

I'm reading Nietzsche, and he most avidly opposes the state of man as an instrument where his so-called virtues (chastity, diligence, obedience) are used in the service of others. He abhors the idea that such virtues be used as a "public utility" to the destruction of the "highest private end." Nietzsche would most certainly not encourage one to dance.

It is not too much to ask oneself, after each act or accomplishment, if one has learned something. Whatever the passion from joy to despair, if something has been learned and one subsequently acquires at least a meager sense of progress, then everything has been worthwhile. So I ask myself, what did I learn in rehearsal, the rehearsal that was momentary joy but left me with a weakness of spirit? I got a few corrections here and there, and there was the ever-present pleasure of watching Suzanne and Balanchine at work. But what did I really learn of lasting value?

I learned, as one does in every rehearsal every day, that life goes on and rehearsal begins and ends no matter how despairing one may feel about such probabilities. I learned about the art of spending an hour with a peace derived from practice. How did I learn about this? By repetition and practice, like an animal. The only part my mind played was in formulating the learning into thought. I was an instrument going through the motions. Learning by way of repetition and routine is an avoidance and a waste of the human being's greatest gift of all—the gift of thought.

I like to think that dancing is the highest endeavor I could ever attempt. Perhaps I feel this so strongly because of its difficulty. Surely if I could conquer every whim and passion and desire that is detrimental to my dancing, it would be an accomplishment. And so am I judging dancing as my highest endeavor because if I crush three-fourths of my spirit I may succeed? What total idiocy! The thought that one is achieving something worthwhile by the very act of disregarding one's passions!

I have been seduced by the social world. I met one new face, and I met ten more. I have not taken a "class" this week —i.e., I have not examined myself in the mirror (and therefore have not been both blinded by my self-analysis and reviled by my limits).

January 25: Which comes first—the theater or life? I could not help wondering tonight as I lay on the stage in *Firebird.* I am a monster, a butterfly monster. I'm in a splotchy green unitard with white gloves, gauze wings and uneven bosoms. For the most part I am blinded by my big white mask, which offers a profile as the face. When it is essential for me to see where I am going, I grab the wire netting in my mouth and hold on for dear life.

As the Firebird cast her spell over the monster kingdom, I lay on my back—downstage, on stage left. She quietly walked amongst us as the music rose softly and serenely. I looked up at the black dome of the theater, the blackness broken by the faint lights of the huge chandelier and the surrounding lights of the tiers. It was like a church. It was like the sky at night. How I adored my vision! The theater is a re-creation of the universe, and on the stage we perform a re-creation of life. I prayed that my perspective would never be so distorted by this theater life that I would forget that the source of beauty and spiritualism lies in nature. I'll never have to renounce that, although one day I will re-nounce the vision I had tonight—that of the lights of the theater as seen from the stage.

January 27: Last night was truly great. We did the finale of *Stars and Stripes* to celebrate the return of the hostages from Iran. The audience applauded throughout and gave us a standing ovation at the end. The house lights were turned on, and for the first time ever the audience had equal status with the performers. We met at the footlights of the stage, waving, clapping and shouting at one another. Two worlds brought together by a common aim.

Why am I so afraid to leave NYCB? I could probably return. Certainly I could always return to dancing, if dancing indeed again became my desire. This clinging to NYCB must be born of routine and habit. I grew into it, fell into it. I did not choose it, for I had no alternatives. Now I must choose. What is this false idea that the New York City

Ballet alone is dancing itself? Dancing is not NYCB (but I retain grave doubts about such a truth), dancing is within me. I can dance whenever and wherever and however I choose. But I must have more knowledge than I have now in order to choose.

Dancing is not essential to my life, but I act as if it were, clinging with a dreadful desperation that surely cannot help its growth! Do I have the courage to question and discard the only security I know in order to find one greater and more lasting?

January 28: I'm in the dressing room, just after *Raymonda Variations,* with the sweat still dripping over my powdered cheeks and my sore old feet propped up. I was lousy.

A few of us dancers—girls—just had a long-drawn-out after-performance meal. As usual we ended up on the endlessly fascinating and obvious topic: New York City Ballet and its members. We skip from new company members to old and new stars. We don't discuss their dancing; we've all seen it and know it. What is so fascinating is what has happened, is happening and will happen to their careers. True merit is not the only deciding factor. Intrigues, love affairs, manipulations, timing and idiosyncrasies decide everyone's life and future. That each and every member is a fantastically strong and good dancer—soloist material in any other company—is taken for granted. We pose the question of what would happen if everyone received his fair due of recognition. Absolute chaos—everyone would be a soloist. So the inevitable result of having a company of soloists as corps members is both the greatest dance company in the world and a great deal of misery and frustration. As I've said, the high point of most of our careers is just before we enter the company!

Offhand I try to think of who comes to mind as a satisfied, smiling dancer. Only two or three out of a hundred and five. But there are also only a few true miseries. The rest lie somewhere in between. So what conclusion have I reached? Dancing is like life, and like all professions in life, the good and the bad and pure happiness are rare on a lasting basis. Dare I defy all example and say I want only joy and believe it is possible?

I have a friend, another dancer. She is in the company. A girl, a woman maybe, at least on the cusp of transition. She is worried, removed, dejected, tormented. One day she speaks, the next she is silent, the third she scowls, the fourth she shouts, and the fifth she recoils back into her shell.

Her hips hurt. They are narrow and not made to turn out. They look cute and sexy, like a boy's, like a little kid's. But they hurt her. Sometimes she says so, but whether she does or not it always shows on her face. She works very hard. She sweats and groans and pants and puffs. She bends over and caves in after she jumps.

She worries about the future, about time, and she wonders how to beat them—to beat time and to beat her body before they beat her to it. Who will win? Does she want fame? She is a little bit famous already; does she want more? Does she have too much of what she does not want, and too little of what she does want? Is she a prisoner within her hips, their pain and her small frame?

She says she is hungry, but she can never eat much. Her stomach is small and fights. It is like a hard ball of fibers and sinews, knotted.

But she must dance. She has a contract. Still her hips hurt.

January 30: True elegance entered the theater tonight with the return of *Vienna Waltzes*. Spirits were high. *Vienna Waltzes* entails no difficult dancing and no overt body exposure and always ends the evening. Hence we are free, free from all "technique" anxieties. Our only aim is beauty, extreme, stylized beauty. The makeup room is full of girls bejeweling their teased wigs until no hair is visible, adding every possible color variation to their faces. Not one facial cell goes forgotten or unfilled with pink, red and blue sparkles. Powder fills the air, blown aside by the frequent outbursts of laughter as someone discovers yet another exaggerated adornment for her face and neck.

Backstage was full of smiling faces and the oddball waltzing girls in the hallway dressed only in their bathrobes. The music is infectious. I can't help thinking of the undeniable joy everyone derives from old-fashioned elegance—long silk gowns and ballroom dancing with a partner, set steps and an orchestra. Why oh why do we not indulge in such spirit-raising events more often? Those crazy all-night discos with neon lights, deafening rock music and the smell of pot are no substitute. I can't imagine any greater drug than bedecking oneself with silk gowns and ostrich feathers and dancing with a man in a tuxedo.

When he wanted to dazzle his audience completely he would suddenly and unexpectedly spring from the ground, whirling his two legs about each other with bewildering swiftness in the air, as if it were trilling with them, and then, with a subdued bump, which nevertheless shook everything within him to its depths, returned to earth.

— *Thomas Mann*, "Tonio Kröger"

I just read a review of a new book by a dancer that attempts to get inside a dancer's mind. That it seems not to have succeeded too well is not surprising. Our minds are as different from one another as anyone else's. Also, I guess, you have to be an unhappy dancer to write at all. If I were totally at peace dancing, I would have nothing to say. Those moments of pure silent inner joy and peace have no words and do not demand any thoughts. A happy dancer is silent, and proof of his or her peace is in that silence, devoid of all need to talk.

What goes through my head when I am onstage dancing? I hear the music, see the lights—lights everywhere, in the wings, on the roof and in the audience. On occasion a face stands out clearly, but more often I get the strange glaring reflection from eyeglasses. I feel my toes and legs and stomach and back and arms and neck and head and eyes. There are no thoughts, no words, just total physical awareness and control.

What puts it all together? Instinct, I suppose; a sense of beauty and style and appropriateness, a sort of unformulated image that the music and costumes and steps all combine to suggest. The music climaxes, and one's movements climax. The music is soft and sweet, and one is soft and mellow. The music quickens, and one is sprightly, clear and distinct. We simply react to the music, and our technique, strength and knowledge enable us to react in a classical style. We have learned a large repertoire of movements, and they are second nature by now. No words or thoughts happen on stage.

A friend—more than a friend—arrives in my life from France, and the impossibilities of the dancing life become ever clearer. I am at the theater six days a week for twelve hours a day. What love could ever grow? I speed in and out of the house to class, rehearsals and performance. To say I am torn is an understatement.

This reminds me of a conversation I overheard yesterday: "Tell him I really like him and like talking to him, but my dancing comes first, that's all, so I can't go out." Our lives in a nutshell. The impossibility of combining love, life and dancing is so obvious. Compromises can bring only mediocrity in both areas. And who wants a mediocre dancer or a mediocre love affair!

Dancing may be my whole life thus far, but after I hear myself say, confiding to a friend, "This is the first time I've been happy through and through all season," I wonder about the purpose of life. If simple happiness is the aim, dancing is not the business. If beauty, growth and dedication are worthier objects, then dancing stands a chance. I suppose I believe in the second, but my whole earthly body and mind never stop demanding simple joy. And so each night I rush home for a few hours of love and joy and talk. I can see my own desperation. Grab it now, tonight, for it will be gone tomorrow and you will not follow it. And so while I stuff down a corn muffin for lunch and dream of escaping, the sound of banging toe shoes and complaints about the casting echo in my ears. Dancing may not be the perfect substitute for love, human love, but it certainly requires all the time and thought and energy that could otherwise be dedicated to love.

I met a girl last night who recently left the New York City Ballet after many years. She bubbled with life; she smiled and laughed as never before. She was open and warm and giving. I asked her curiously, "How's life out there?" She is tap-dancing and singing and acting and auditioning and having love affairs around every corner. She was a happy and tempting sight after knowing her always with-drawn and sad and alone, always alone.

I can see no way, no way at all, to be a woman and dance. When I was five pounds thinner with no monthly cycles, I was more constant in mood. But this fluctuation and the desires that often come in cycles now distract all my thoughts and weaken my ability to dance. I know those feelings should be my equipment and my uniqueness on stage, but they are not, not now; they only frighten and inhibit me. Perhaps they are so new I have not yet come to terms with them. How can I work, how can I stand at the barre every morning and every night, when one day is an ecstasy and the next an agony?

I light up a cigarette and begin to read the article on Kyra Nichols in the Arts and Leisure section of *The New York Times*. Her life, her family and Balanchine. I speed through the article and feel strongly the power and mystique of the fame it reflects. I latch onto every word from Balanchine, helplessly and selfishly relating it to my own demise at NYCB. Perhaps I don't work enough. One thing is sure: I have no straight vision as do the Kyra Nicholses of ballet. My life is bigger and more complicated than dancing now. I cannot leave questions unanswered and just go to the barre. Ah, what a story Kyra Nichols could tell about dancing. But she has neither the time nor the need to scribble as I do.

February 8: It is Sunday, exactly one week until the end of the season, and the end of a phase, a three-month phase. Our lives are sectioned by seasons, dancing seasons. And I will end the season with a friend who is also a lover, but best of all a friend. And so dancing is beautiful. I can work quietly and consistently, and the stage is more than beautiful —it is the celebration of my new peace. It tastes of the love I feel. So now I know it was not dancing that was hurting me, but a lack of something else. I am not the first nor will I be the last who wishes to stop dancing because of the loneliness.

Week of February 10: I am happy dancing. Why? It's the end of the season, vacation pay came in today, and I'm writing in the cozy curve of another body.

We had hysterics on stage tonight, sixteen convulsed bodies and red faces from the girls in Act III of *Coppélia*.

The roach was first detected on far stage left by he who was nearest. The word traveled faster than the roach. During the pas de deux, the roach twisted in circles and made no forward progress. (No doubt the shining lights confused his sense of direction as much as they do ours.) But as the first variation began, he gained some sense of purpose and raced across to stage right. He learned fast, hit the center line and followed it straight downstage as Patty McBride did her turning pas de bourrée step. We thought sure death was in sight, but he survived all the way to the headlights. Someone suggested he really was interested in music, not dancing, contesting our verdict that he châiné-ed very well indeed and that only Patty could maintain more balance. But he could not cross the dividing line and panicked into the footlights.

A thought on dancing: We were discussing life. What is the proof of life? Movement. And what higher and more beautiful movement is there than dancing? We use our bodies to manifest life itself.

As the last day of rehearsals approaches, we have only replacements to rehearse, and the atmosphere is relaxed. The end is in sight, both of this dancing season and of my journal. The problem of an appropriate ending plagues me. Should my story not end one year later as I have a lucky break and become overnight the talk of the ballet world? Would that not somehow put all my worries into a most curious and wonderful perspective? But this is the story of a season, not a career; of a phase, not an entirety.

What have I not recorded? My favorite ballets to watch, to dance? They are the same. I love them all; they are all different, all special, all unique. *Serenade* is sacred. It has so much dancing, such beautiful music, mysterious lighting, evocative moods, romance and lovely costumes—it is perfect. *Concerto Barocco* is a full emotional and physical experience in twenty minutes—onstage the whole time, sparely dressed, purity of movement, technique and speed. It is so simple, so spare. Along with *Apollo* this ballet somehow demands more perfection than others. One simply does not put a foot wrong. It would be blasphemous.

Union Jack—huge, festive, colorful, with those drum rolls that never fail to inject life. No nerves for this ballet; we are well covered in kilts and velvet jackets, pointe work is minimal, and the masses of people on stage are warming and close; a real feeling of "we're in this together." Because of the quick costume change for the sailor section we are allowed a rare privilege. We do not have to hang our costumes up. Instead, we tear off our kilts, camisoles, jackets, berets and sporrans on the way to the dressing room. They are flung on a huge white sheet on the floor. Berets and kilts literally fly across the room. We then collapse on top of the pile to struggle into our sailor pants and lace-up shoes. This change is quite an event in itself, all done while onstage the Pearly King and Queen are twirling their umbrellas.

Vienna Waltzes—the whole thing, but for me doing the polka in a red wig, big high-heeled satin shoes and a minimal bunny outfit is the height of joyous lunacy and has never failed to make me grin for an hour afterwards. It is also perfectly timed so that I can shower, dress and be back in the wings to watch Suzanne in the last waltz.

Raymonda and *Coppélia* had very bad, nervous performances at times, but in the later ones the faults were conquered to double satisfaction! And *Nutcracker* . . . *Nutcracker* had to be taken as a whole. Five weeks, the same parts every night. A lesson in creative resources to be fresh each night. And the snow—the snow is always so beautiful, perhaps the most beautiful time ever to be on stage. *Tchaikovsky Piano Concerto No. 2,* seven performances, a rarity, lots of luscious dancing, bravura, grandeur and always wonderful applause. The energy level is so high, one can feel the air crack with nervousness and excitement.

February 14: It is 8:05, and the curtain is about to go up on *La Source.* Tonight in *Le Bourgeois Gentilhomme* Allegra Kent will make her first and last appearance of the season. The curiosity, love and anticipation we give her is special. It is Valentine's Day, and the theater is filled with chocolates and cake and cookies. Every dressing room, every bench, every table is laden, and hands are grabbing and mouths are chewing as fast as they can.

People are packing as they announce their last performance. Laundry is ordered, and black theater cases are filled. The energy level rises visibly, though this is the time of fatigue.

The surges of family feeling also rise as we all discuss mutual feelings and long for vacations.

February 16: And so last night it ended. We were given enough cakes, cookies, chocolates and wine for an army. A high celebration. We were all lost in the last-minute housewifely turmoil of moving house, running around the theater in borrowed bathrobes all day, lining up for the washing machines. Great groups of kids gathered and talked and competed for the next cycle. Theater cases were sat on, crushed, closed. Makeup and old leotards were hawked or thrown away. Throwing away a detestable leotard is an emotional experience unlike any other!

When the curtain came down on *Western Symphony,* the most animal-like screams of enthusiasm rose from the audience. Cut-up ballet programs were thrown on stage, filling the air with their fluttering (and more than one of us thought that these colored papers were money, perhaps not the purest of thoughts, but so beautifully human of us!).

We threw our eyelashes and shoes into the garbage with glee and smeared the baby oil over our powdered faces for the last time! (In fact every action of that last day was significant and remarked upon as the last—the last ballet, the last warm-up, the last ribbons sewed, the last wash and the last curtain.) The most minuscule act took on dramatic and profound significance as the final one after three long months.

We all agree that we are afraid that when we wake up tomorrow, we will no longer be dancers at all—as if the anticipation of vacation and free time will be absorbed instantly into our muscles and fifteen years of training will disappear.

Our thoughts are now so far away from our twitching muscles that we cannot imagine how the two states can exist simultaneously in one body. The question that we ask ourselves every night is clearer and more frightening as freedom approaches, for we know that unless we are at the barre or on stage we are not dancers but only people.

Dancers have a direct connection to the heavens and the gods—Balanchine and Stravinsky receive their talents and visions from God, and we as their instruments interpret those visions for mortal men. We are their servants. We are creative in the same way that the paint in the pot is creative.

We are the means to the end. We are essential, and we are on display. We receive the applause. Alone we are incapable and stationary. We are not the beginning or the end of creation. We are the innocents of beauty; we wait and listen and pray for guidance.

My thoughts travel on another line. Those who try to create and interpret a vision they receive are the creators—composers, writers, choreographers, painters. They work alone with their minds; they have the time and solitude to reflect and perfect their vision until they decide it is presentable. They retain a power that dancers, musicians and actors do not have. They can choose how and when and where to present their vision. They have the power of time on their side, to choose when they are ready. But we the performers can only do—the moment the curtain rises. For us, all reflections, all thought and all decisions are out of place; it is too late. We must be like trained animals and active instruments, responding to the learned stimulus of music. We must be spontaneous in public in front of three thousand pairs of eyes. The creator need be spontaneous only to himself—alone in his thoughts, his workshop. The audience is our judge, but only God and the creator himself are the judges of his solitary spontaneity.

I am jealous, very jealous, of the privacy a creator is allowed and allows himself. He can go public in his own good time, while we, the instruments, must go public every night at eight o'clock no matter where our thoughts and energies lie. And more often than not my thoughts and desires are halfway around the world—but the curtain rises and the stage seduces, and without fail my thoughts and energies are brought into the moment—the dancing that is my natural reaction.

But still what is dance, and what can steps tell us?

O let us enjoy this lovely action a little while longer in all simplicity! . . . Right, left, forward, backward; and upward and downward, she seems to be offering gifts, perfumes, incense, kisses and her life itself to all the points of the sphere and to the poles of the universe. . . .

She traces roses, lacy patterns, stars of movements, and magic precincts. . . . Barely is a circle closed than she leaps from it. . . . She leaps and runs after phantoms! She picks a flower, and behold! it is only a smile. Oh! how she proclaims her non-existence by means of her inexhaustible lightness!

—*Paul Valéry,* Dance and the Soul

AFTERWORD:
OCTOBER 1981

The tummy is back—flat; the diet is on. Class was great: the energy is infinite, creativity flowed, the discipline worked; order was maintained, and yet there was spontaneity.

I dance, I photograph, I sew, I shop, I read, I eat, I swim, I eat and I dance again.

PRIORITIES:

Dancing
Writing
Friends
Food
Finance

1. Sew shoes
2. Pack theater case
3. Wash leotards

4. Sort makeup
5. Buy mascara
6. Fabulon shoes

Class: I jive, I click, I snap—it's comin', it's goin', it's stoppin', it's happenin'. Okay, slow; easy, faster, harder, faster, fast, fast, fast, fast—fast—faster—fast, fast, fast—RELAX. And stretch—and stretch and stretch over and over and over and relax and relax and relax and relax and finish.

I understand so little of what I know.

The dam of tension and energy is broken, and how I dance! I am living proof of the need each day to clear body and mind—to dance, to sweat. And to stare in the goddamned mirror? You bet. Most people eat too much to dance . . .

Two and a half months after I finished this journal, I took a leave of absence from the New York City Ballet. My every thought and action had led to this point, but the reality was inconceivable. For a while I awakened each morning realizing more and more my need for this freedom. The possibilities seemed endless, and my desire to dance was renewed. The pressure of daily rehearsals, of giving all my time and energy to the uses of NYCB was released, and the lightness I felt was euphoric. For the first time in my life, my future was unplanned, uncontracted for. I had neither work nor school on my agenda. I felt gaily arrogant.

Can the pain of five years be lifted?
The fouettés—can they return?

The confidence to carry the beauty, can it excite again?
Can the overwork of the worker be removed from
the body—from the face?

And so I left, and now I am back. Eleven months after this diary was begun I have indeed executed what I thought would forever be only a wish. I wanted to leave, and I was terrified to. Now I have returned. What have I learned?

I was spoiled in my agony, however real the pain. I had to leave to see what I had left. I will never forget an evening in a pub in Cambridge, England. A scientist, an American, said to me, "I hear you're a dancer. I guess you don't dance for Balanchine, ha-ha." When I told him I did, it was like a bomb exploding. He announced to the entire bar, "This young woman dances for Balanchine."

"Who is Balanchine?" someone asked.

"He is probably the only creative genius alive."

I felt tremendously proud—until I remembered that I had renounced dancing, renounced Balanchine and had no claim to this pride. It made me think again.

I went away and did all the things that belong to the so-called living I had longed for, but they seemed somehow unsatisfactory. My pleasure at meals was only momentary; I had a full belly and no need for those kilocalories. I was grandiose in appearance and minuscule in substance.

I found myself "selling Balanchine" to everyone I encountered, spreading the gospel I had betrayed. I found the idea of living was misleading: one is what one does, and my wish for pure being was meaningless garble. I was incapable of restraining my energies, but I had nowhere to direct them.

I wanted to dance. I talked about dancing, defended dancing and justified dancing. I became a prophet of the dance—to myself—an inactive missionary of ballet. I slowly realized that I was a hypocrite, and then I knew that it could be only a matter of days or weeks before I would have to return.

I simply could not give in to myself after twelve years of discipline and restraint and reward. I forgave myself each day—at least I tried.

And so I returned, perhaps guided, just as I had been twelve years earlier, by the refusal to accept the pain caused by a threat of being unable to dance.

I was ornate when I left. I returned simplified. Today I am full of hopes and goals and a faith that is all the stronger for having been lost. My thoughts have changed direction. Before, when I tired in a class or onstage, I took it as one more sign of failure, of weakness, of proof that I was wrong to be dancing and trying and caring so very much. Now when I tire, I think of how to overcome it, how to work through it and conquer it. I do my best and forgive myself for the rest. I try to envision myself, not Gelsey Kirkland. Before, when a toe hurt, I let it bleed. Now I stop and wash and bandage it.

I have discovered the bliss of total immersion, total concentration in dancing. As self-consciousness lessens, the possibility of concentration increases. Ironically, it is only when one loses all sense of others that it is possible to please them. Is that the element of beauty?

I am in the coffee shop as always, at the counter because all the tables are full. It is lunchtime. A young dancer and her boyfriend attract attention with a soft, smacking kiss. I feel instantly alone in contrast to their closeness, and I scribble all the more . . . But there is a strength, a lonely joy, in knowing that I too have had my day of kisses. Does one become used to this lonely splendor too easily?

We are just back from a week of dancing in Fort Worth. I am amazed at the change in my ways, my dancing ways, from the sad and slow to the open and energetic by sheer force of will and conscious decision. I tell myself to turn, and turn I do. I wonder while I dance how I can find the peace and quiet to write. I'm bubbling with energy.

When there is no performance, the purpose of life is class: to give one's all at 9:30 A.M., 10:30, 11:00, 11:30. As always, class proves a challenge beyond everything. Today I triumph; yesterday I did not. But back I go every day, however much fear I generate to deter me. I was not great— perhaps not even good—but I worked through the fears. I could not believe it. It is safe to live in one's own well-worn groove where one is comfortable with one's chosen limits, chosen measurements of success and failure. But today as I pirouetted straight through the limits, I knew I could do more and then more again. For one triumph leads to another, on into infinity. How far can I go? How far will I go?

I can feel so improved, and then one glimpse in the mirror and I am disillusioned. How can I contain such contradictions?

Life is simpler now, and all my energy is directed one way, instead of twenty. It is hard to decide which action of mine made the deepest difference. Leaving NYCB? That day was so simple and easy. A few words, and out I walked into a euphoria that put all my former triumphs to shame. It lasted three days; then I began to pay my dues.

Now the cycle is complete. I probably always knew that it would be. But the return was unimaginable. I left with such relief. I am hesitant to speak about my return. It is an ongoing procedure. I have a joy and an energy and I fear explanations. I don't want to examine them too deeply or search out the sources. Joy is a gift, and I will not look for a price tag. Joy produces action. My natural state is not passive. I am a dancer.

I have returned and the company is the same. I like that. I change enough.